D0994284

CHRISTIANITY
EXPLORED
YOUTH EDITION

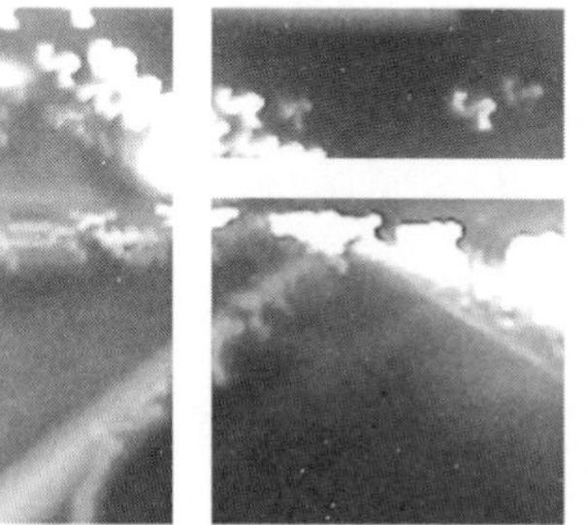

CY

CY: The Youth Edition of Christianity Explored was developed by
Barry Cooper, Matthew Seymour and Sam Shammas in association with Young Life (UK).

www.christianityexplored.com
www.younglife.org.uk

CY Leader's Guide

Printed 2006, reprinted 2007.
Published by:
The Good Book Company Ltd
Elm House, 37 Elm Road, New Malden, Surrey KT3 3HB, UK
Tel: 0845 225 0880; Fax: 0845 225 0990
email: admin@thegoodbook.co.uk
website: www.thegoodbook.co.uk

The Good Book Company

ISBN-13: 9781905564446

Design by Sandbar Mary
Cover Design by Diane Bainbridge
Cartoons and Illustrations by Alex Webb-Peploe
Printed in China by Prosperous Printing House, ICTI Registration No. ICTI-00946

CY
LEADER'S GUIDE

This seven-week course is designed to present young people with the good news about Jesus. With a creative mixture of Bible studies, talks, DVDs, activities and group discussions, ***CY*** takes your youth group on a journey through Mark's Gospel. They'll **CY Jesus Matters**, **CY Jesus Died**, **CY Jesus Lives** - and much more.

What makes this course - and the Christian gospel - distinctive is its insistence on God's remarkable grace: the clear teaching that although we human beings have rebelled against God, we are deeply loved by him. Loved with an outrageous, costly and incomprehensible love that was poured out for us on a little hill just outside Jerusalem.

It may be no easier for leaders to relate Jesus' teaching on sin, judgement, wrath and hell than it is for a course participant to hear it. But, if we are prepared to trust in the Holy Spirit's power to open blind eyes, these uncomfortable truths pave the way for a faithful, fruitful life driven by God's grace.

This *Leader's Guide* is divided into three sections: the first will introduce you to how the course works; the second will train you to use the course; and the third will be your guide each week as you actually run the course.

SECTION 1
SETTING UP THE COURSE

SECTION 2
TRAINING NOTES

SECTION 3

USER GUIDE

This section is intended for the main course leader – the person responsible for organizing the course and delivering the talks. If you are not the main course leader, go to Section 2: Training Notes, which will prepare you to lead people through ***CY***.

SECTION 1
SETTING UP THE COURSE

SETTING UP THE COURSE
GETTING STARTED

Telling young people about Jesus Christ is a stunning privilege and a huge responsibility.

It's a stunning privilege because Almighty God is pleased to call us his "fellow workers" (1 Corinthians 3:9) as he seeks and saves the lost. And it's a huge responsibility because it can be tempting to present a watered-down gospel that has no power to save and is "no gospel at all" (Galatians 1:7).

CY has been developed to let the gospel tell the gospel: it takes you, and those in your care, on a journey through Mark's Gospel to discover who Jesus is, why he came and what it means to follow him.

To help your journey run smoothly, you will need to consider the following before the course begins.

WHERE SHOULD YOU MEET?

Find somewhere where your group will be happy to invite their friends. You may like to experiment with some different locations other than church premises. Avoid using a classroom or somewhere that looks like one so that people don't feel they are back at school.

The environment can have a big impact on people's willingness to get involved in activities and discussion, so be creative in the way you decorate and set up the room.

It's important to choose a place where you are unlikely to be interrupted and where you will be able to meet every week at the same time.

HOW OFTEN SHOULD YOU MEET?

As this is a seven-week course, once a week for seven weeks is the ideal. Because each week builds on the one before, try not to interrupt the regular schedule of the meetings.

There's also a weekend or day away that takes place between Weeks 6 and 7, called "***CY*** We're Not Alone". In some youth evangelism there has been too much emphasis on "getting people to pray the prayer", with little opportunity for serious consideration of what is involved in following Jesus. As Christians, our aim should be to work for "fruit that will last" (John 15:16), not a superficial religious experience that is quickly forgotten when life gets tough. With that in mind, this time away sets out the implications of becoming a Christian, so that young people can adequately "count the cost" before making a commitment.

WHAT'S INVOLVED IN EACH WEEK?

The structure is the same each week: Food; Group Activity; EXPLORE (Bible study); Talk / DVD; TALKBACK (group discussion).

Below is the suggested duration for each component:

Food	30 minutes
Group Activity	25 minutes
EXPLORE	25 minutes
Talk / DVD	20 minutes
TALKBACK	20 minutes

You should be able to complete each week in 2 hours. This can be shortened if necessary by limiting the time taken for food, activities or discussion.

It is important to watch the time taken for each of these components. Over-running can cause frustration and boredom – and may make it difficult for you to communicate the gospel effectively.

CY has been extensively piloted with groups all over the world and the current course is the result of detailed feedback. We would urge you, when you first run the course, to try and use it as written – you may be surprised by how well your group handles the activities and questions!

FOOD

The main reason that food is included is not as a device to get young people to come (although in our experience, teenagers will go anywhere for free food!). Rather, it is because as you sit or stand around eating, you and your fellow leaders have the opportunity to interact with the young people – to discover what they are like, what interests them, what struggles and difficulties they face.

Time is precious, so if you can, recruit outside help with the food so that you are free to spend time with the group members. Resist the temptation to make the food over-elaborate. Keep it simple to eat and clear away. (Although it's always good to make an effort, there is a danger that food can end up squeezing out time for exploring the gospel.)

GROUP ACTIVITY

This is a short, fun game, intended to introduce the theme of the week, and build relationships between people. Each week you will need to make sure you have all the equipment needed to run the activity.

EXPLORE

This is a Bible study from Mark's Gospel, giving the group a chance to explore Jesus' life and teaching.

The skill of your fellow leaders is crucial during EXPLORE – an excellent reason for you to schedule some training time for them. Section 2: Training Notes is specially designed to help you do this training.

TALK OR DVD

At this point you, as the course leader, will deliver a short talk (see "Preparing the Talks" for talk outlines).

Alternatively, during weeks 2-7, you can use the ***Christianity Explored*** DVD Series instead of doing a "live" talk. (Note: Although the DVDs work very well for Weeks 2-7, they are not designed to be used for ***CY*** Week 1 or the ***CY*** Weekend / Day Away.)

If you are using the DVDs, make sure that your leaders have watched them beforehand so that there will be no surprises with the content.

Because the DVDs feature on-screen Bible text, it is inadvisable to use them with large groups unless you have access to a projection screen and projector. Please also note that you'll need to stop the DVD before the questions appear at the end of each programme as these are not designed to work with ***CY***.

TALKBACK

This is a chance to discuss the themes of the talk, and bring out the implications. TALKBACK questions are particularly designed to draw out what your group members actually believe.

HOW WILL YOU INVITE PEOPLE?

Encourage your youth group to invite their friends. (You might want to do a study with them on the importance of evangelism before you start running ***CY***.) "Friends bringing friends" is the main reason people come to the course.

If you are running ***CY*** as part of a church youth group, you can advertise the course in your church bulletin, during the Sunday services, and at your regular youth group meetings.

Any publicity material you produce about the course needs to reassure people that no-one will be expected to pray, sing or do anything that makes them feel uncomfortable or embarrassed. It is also important to be honest about exactly what will happen, so that people don't feel duped into coming.

It is our hope that the course would not be a "one-time" event, but rather a regular feature of your calendar. And once your youth group have experienced ***CY***, you'll find that they'll be eager to invite their friends to future courses.

WHO WILL LEAD?

We recommend that one leader is made responsible for delivering all the talks, or introducing the DVDs, and running the evening. If the group is small, the same leader will lead the group through EXPLORE and TALKBACK.

If you have a large group, you will need to split participants into smaller groups and find additional leaders to lead EXPLORE and TALKBACK with each group. Participants should stay with the same leader(s) every week. We recommend a maximum of 8 young people per group, with at least two leaders per group.

All leaders should be Christians who are able to teach, encourage discussion and care for participants. They should be able to teach the Bible faithfully and clearly – and be able to deal with difficult questions on Mark's Gospel. Participants may have questions that are not explicitly dealt with in the material, so leaders should have enough general biblical knowledge to help participants with these questions. (For help on answering difficult questions, see www.christianityexplored.com/reading)

Leaders should also be able to handle pastoral situations with care and sensitivity. In a mixed group, it is vital to have both male and female leaders present, in order to deal with pastoral situations appropriately.

It can be very effective to ask Christian young people to lead EXPLORE. The most important qualities of a leader are not age, but maturity and gifting. Asking a suitable young person to lead may encourage greater discussion and debate. If you do take this route, having an older Christian present in the group (but not leading the discussion) will be helpful in dealing with difficult situations or hard questions. It's also a good idea to choose a young leader who has already been through ***CY*** as a participant.

WHAT WILL YOU NEED TO RUN CY?

Everyone on the course – leaders and participants – will need to be given a Bible. For the sake of clarity, it is important that everyone uses the same version. The version used throughout the course material is the New International Version (NIV). If you choose to use another version, please check carefully that the wording of the questions makes sense against the Bible version you are using. We recommend that you use complete Bibles during the course, rather than just a Gospel of Mark, or a New Testament. This helps familiarize your group with all of God's word, emphasizes that the whole of Scripture is God-breathed, and will mean that they have the whole Bible to take away with them at the end of the course.

Each participant should be given a copy of the ***CY*** *User Guide* which contains the EXPLORE studies, space to write their answers, talk summaries and room to make notes. We recommend that these are kept by the leaders and handed out each week. (When you collect them after TALKBACK, you will need to promise that their *User Guides* are private and that the leaders won't be reading them! Explain that you're holding on to them so that they won't be forgotten next week.)

HOW SHOULD YOU PRAY FOR CY?

Nothing happens unless God is at work, so make sure that you give plenty of time to prayer. Try to recruit prayer partners among your Christian friends, or from your church congregation, who will commit themselves to praying before (and during) the course.

- Pray for the preparation of the talks – that they would be faithful to God's word, passionate, challenging and clear.
- Pray for the leaders – that they would be well prepared and that they would "watch their life and doctrine closely" (1 Timothy 4:16).
- Pray for the young people – that many would attend; that by his Spirit, God would open their eyes to see who Jesus is, and by his Spirit give them the desire to turn and follow him.

Please let us know when and where your course is running! The ***CY*** Team would love to pray for you. Email cy@christianityexplored.com or write to the General Manager, ***Christianity Explored***, All Souls Church, Langham Place, London W1B 3DA, United Kingdom.

SETTING UP THE COURSE

PREPARING THE TALKS

After food, the group activity and EXPLORE, the talk for that week is delivered. (Section 3: User Guide contains all the information you need to run the activities and EXPLORE studies for each week.)

This chapter contains talk outlines to help you prepare your talks. The outlines give you the basis of the talk, so you can then add your own illustrations, examples and applications that may be particularly relevant to your group.

We strongly recommend that one person does all the talks. This gives continuity to the "voice" and makes it less likely that valuable elements are left out of the teaching.

Remember to keep your talk relatively short. We recommend 20 minutes maximum.

To download the talk outlines, visit www.christianityexplored.com/cy

OUTLINE OF TALK 1
CY IT'S WORTH EXPLORING

This first talk must be delivered "live" – do not use programme 1 of the **Christianity Explored** *DVD Series. Encourage people to write notes on the UPLOAD page in their* User Guide.

AIM

- To welcome people to the course.
- To make the point that many people have the wrong impression of Christianity because they don't have all the information they need.
- To explain that Christianity is not about rules or ceremony. It's all about Jesus Christ.
- To explain that we can only find true significance and real meaning in our lives once we realize that there's a God who created us and who wants us to know him.
- To explain that we can only get to know God through Jesus, and that we're going to find out about him on ***CY***.

OPENING

Share your own experience of how you viewed Christianity before you became a Christian and how you formed that opinion. Maybe an embarrassing and funny church experience you had.

So, when you think of Christianity, what things come into your mind? Rules and regulations? A bad church experience when you were younger? What did you draw on your poster? [*See page 100 for details of this activity.*]

Talk about some of the things that were drawn on the poster. Don't refer to the people who drew them, or make judgements about the views of Christianity that were expressed. Just say that these views are very common; lots of people think this way. But these views are not based on all the information.

But remember the very first sentence of Mark: he says that Christianity isn't really about any of those things.

1. WHAT IS CHRISTIANITY ALL ABOUT?

Read Mark 1:1 aloud.

- Christianity is not really about rules or ceremony, or being a good human being. It's actually about a person – Jesus Christ, who Mark says is the Son of God.
- The word "gospel" means "good news". So Mark is telling us that the gospel – the good news, Christianity – is all about Jesus Christ.
- Now, if you talk to people about the big questions in life, there are two that come up again and again: "Where did life come from?" and "What is the point of life?"

2. WHERE DID LIFE COME FROM?

- Scientists spend billions every year trying to work out how the earth began and where life came from. I think most people would like to know the answer to that question, don't you?
- And there are really only two answers you can give: either we're here by chance; or we were created by someone or something.
- Maybe we're here just by chance – the product of some atoms and some molecules that have appeared out of nothing and then come together, spun around, exploded and brought the whole world into being. By accident. Now if that's true, just think about the consequences of that. You see, if we are accidents, if [name someone in the room – preferably a leader] is an accident, then he / she has no significance, no value. He / she doesn't matter because they're nothing more than a splodge of atoms in a body!
- But if we're made by someone, if we are created and we are someone's workmanship, then we matter enormously. So if [the person you mentioned] isn't a collision of atoms but is actually someone who is made by God in the image of God, in God's likeness, then he / she matters enormously.
- Now that's really important. It means that we don't matter because of our grades, our popularity or our clothes. We don't matter because of where we hang out or the music we've got on our iPod. It means we matter because God has made us and we're made in his image. We have value because we are made by God. Our lives mean something.

3. WHAT IS THE POINT OF LIFE?

- But what exactly is the point of life? People are looking for answers to this question in so many places, but few find an answer that satisfies them.

➡ *You may want to use the following illustration (or come up with another illustration that is particularly relevant to your group about how life without purpose or meaning is empty):* Kurt Cobain was the lead singer of Nirvana. He came to fame in 1991 with the song "Smells Like Teen Spirit". By 1992, he was married, had a wife and a young child. It was all going so well for him. He was a world-famous singer, he'd made millions of dollars, he had everything – the house, the money, the cars, a wife and a child. And then the following year, he was in a drug detox programme trying to get off some very, very serious drugs. Within the next twelve months Kurt Cobain had committed suicide. Now Kurt Cobain was looking for fulfilment in life. He had all those possessions, he had all those things going for him, he had everything – but he didn't feel he had enough to live for. Why?

- Well, the Bible says that we don't really start living until we know God. You see if I'm made by God, in God's image, the only way I can find what life is really about is to know the one who's made me and to live as he made me to live.
- So, the question is, how can we know God?

4. GETTING TO KNOW GOD

➡ *You may want to use the following illustration (or come up with another illustration that is particularly relevant to your group):* What would you do if you really wanted to know David Beckham? *[or insert another well known personality to suit your group]* You might fly to Spain, stand outside Real Madrid's stadium, scream his name, try to see him. You might try sending him an email or phoning him, but he probably doesn't have a phone number you can find very easily. If you actually want to know David Beckham, you probably need *him* to phone you up and say "[insert name of someone from your group], I want you to come to my next match. I'm going to fly you over on my private jet to Madrid. There will be tickets waiting for you when you get to the stadium. And when the game finishes you can come and see me, and we can chill out with the guys from the team." So really, for us to get to know David Beckham, we need him to *want* to know us.

- The same is true for us and our relationship with God. We can't get to know God unless he wants to know us. And the Bible says he does want to know us: that's why he sent his Son, Jesus Christ. That's why Jesus is good news.

CONCLUSION

On ***CY*** we're going to spend some time exploring who Jesus is. Is he just a man, just a great teacher, just a Galilean carpenter, or is he God himself come down to earth to meet us? Then we're going to look at why he came. Why did he break into history and spend 33 years on earth? And then we're going to ask a further question: what does it mean to follow him? What is it actually like to be a Christian? That's where we're going on ***CY***.

So is this course worth sticking with for seven weeks? The reason I think you'll find it's worth doing is because Jesus answers those two big questions we've been thinking about: where did life come from and what is the point of life? That's why it's worth exploring.

So will you come back next week and ***CY*** Jesus Matters?

Sit with your group and work through TALKBACK.

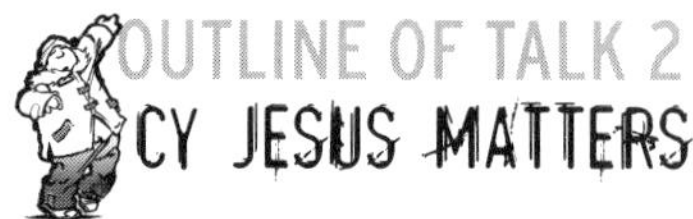

OUTLINE OF TALK 2
CY JESUS MATTERS

You can use the **Christianity Explored** *DVD Series programme 2 for this week, or use the outline below to develop your own talk. Encourage people to write notes on the UPLOAD page in their* User Guide.

AIM

- To show that Jesus is God by exploring five events in Jesus' life that reveal his authority to teach, ability to heal, control of nature, power over death and authority to forgive sins.

OPENING

This week we're going to get to know Jesus. Now, if you wanted to know all about a person from history [*give an example – Elvis, JFK, Winston Churchill, Shakespeare etc*] and what made them tick, the first thing you'd do is look at their life story. So that's what we're going to do, by looking at five important events in Jesus' life and what they tell us about Jesus.

1. JESUS' AUTHORITY TO TEACH

- The first event is in Mark chapter 1, verses 21–22. Why don't we all open our Bibles to that passage and I'll read it aloud for us.

Read aloud Mark 1:21–22.

- What set Jesus apart from other teachers of the law was the way he taught. The other teachers didn't come up with their own material and claimed no authority of their own. Jesus claimed that his words had as much authority as God's words.
- When he speaks, it's as if somebody has suddenly switched on the lights in a dark room. What people heard from the lips of Jesus explained their lives to them. So – can you see in verse 22 – the people were amazed at his teaching.
- But was Jesus all talk? Or did he also walk the walk? The staggering answer is that he did. He said, "Love your enemies and pray for those who persecute

you." Later, as he was being killed, he prayed for his executioners, "Father, forgive them, for they do not know what they are doing." Now that is practicing what you preach!

- So Jesus had the authority to teach, but was he just a teacher?

2. JESUS' ABILITY TO HEAL

- Please look at chapter 1, verses 30–31.

Read aloud Mark 1:30–31.

You may want to use the following illustration: Now have you ever heard a story about someone being healed? You know those types of stories: "Well, I couldn't quite bend my left arm properly. But gradually over the course of time I managed to bend it from here to here. It's a miracle!"

- But this is very different. This woman has a fever and Jesus takes her by the hand and immediately she's made well. And he does that without any medicine, without any doctors, without medical help, and no injections. He heals her just like that.
- Jesus had the ability to heal instantly and miraculously, but was he just a healer?

3. JESUS' CONTROL OF NATURE

- Let's turn to Mark chapter 4 and I'll read from verse 35.

Read aloud Mark 4:35–38.

- What you've got here is a full-blown storm. You're in a boat, you're a fisherman, there are no life jackets, there are no lifeboats to call out, the shore is a long way away and if you sink you are going to die. So it's a serious situation. The disciples say, "Teacher, don't you care if we drown?" Now, if Jesus *is* just a teacher, what on earth can he do about the storm? If he's just a teacher, then they are in terrible trouble, aren't they?
- But is he more than that? Let's see.

Read aloud Mark 4:39–41.

- When Jesus says, “Quiet! Be still!” the wind dies down and the waves stop immediately – it is “completely calm”. Because Jesus has control over nature he can do this. The disciples are terrified – they say, “Who is this? Even the wind and the waves obey him!” Well, whoever he is, he has control over nature.
- Then, in the next chapter, the disciples witness something that is even more astonishing...

4. JESUS' POWER OVER DEATH

- It's in Mark chapter 5 and I'll start reading at verse 21.

➲ *Read aloud Mark 5:21–24.*

- Here is Jairus' daughter who is very ill. Jairus is a synagogue ruler, so he's a powerful man. But he is powerless to do anything for his daughter. He comes to Jesus and he's desperate because his daughter is dying.

➲ *You may want to share a story of a family you know who were devastated by terminal illness, to illustrate Jairus' feelings of helplessness and desperation.*

- So Jairus turns to Jesus. And Jesus goes with him to his house. We pick up the story at verse 35.

➲ *Read aloud Mark 5:35–36.*

- So Jesus has gone with Jairus but he has then been delayed by another event. He's been speaking and then these men come from Jairus' house and they say this to him: “Your daughter is dead.” Then they say, “Why bother the teacher any more?” But Jesus, ignoring what they say, tells the synagogue ruler, “Don't be afraid; just believe.” Now, you've got to be absolutely sure of yourself before you say something like that to someone whose loved one has just died. Because if you're messing around and you're not going to do something truly miraculous, you're just playing with people's feelings.

➲ *Read aloud Mark 5:37–42.*

- So Jesus doesn't just talk the talk. He takes this girl who is dead, and brings her back to life by taking her hand and speaking to her. No electric shocks to get her heart going, just a hand and just a word and the corpse gets up and walks around. So who *is* Jesus if he can do that?

- Well, there's one last event I'd like us to look at. Another piece of evidence as to who Jesus is...

5. JESUS' AUTHORITY TO FORGIVE SINS

- We've read this already in our groups but let's look at it again. It's in Mark chapter 2, verses 1–7, where Jesus heals the paralyzed man.

Read aloud Mark 2:1–7.

- The final piece of evidence about Jesus is that *he alone* can forgive sins. He says to this man, "Son, your sins are forgiven". Now the religious leaders go crazy when he says this. They are furious because they know that only God can forgive sins. So when Jesus says "your sins are forgiven", what he's actually saying is: "I'm God, who is the only one who can forgive sins."

You may want to use the following illustration: Let's imagine I punch [a leader's name] in the stomach, and then I say to [someone else in the room] "Do you forgive me for punching them in the stomach?". That would be pointless, because I punched [leader] in the stomach, so only they can forgive me.

- Now sin is breaking God's commands. Sin is something which offends God. So the one person who can forgive us is not a priest, not some other individual, but only God himself, because it's God who we've offended when we've sinned. So when Jesus says, "Son, your sins are forgiven", he is saying "I'm God."

CONCLUSION

As Jesus teaches, calms the storm, raises the dead, heals the sick and forgives sins – the question we need to ask is: who is Jesus? Is Jesus just a good teacher, just a local carpenter, just a man who lived 2000 years ago who said a few wise things? Or is he God? And if he is God, then can you afford to ignore him?

Sit with your group and work through TALKBACK.

OUTLINE OF TALK 3
WHY JESUS CAME

You can use the **Christianity Explored** *DVD Series programme 3 for this week, or use the outline below to develop your own talk. Encourage people to write notes on the UPLOAD page in their* User Guide.

AIM

- To explain that Jesus came to deal with our biggest problem: our sin.
- To define sin.
- To explain the consequences of sin.
- To show that only Jesus can rescue us from our sin.

OPENING

If you ask people on the street why Jesus came, you'll get many different answers. Some people would say he came to bring peace on earth. Others that he came to cure disease and end the sufferings of the world. And others that he wanted to change society and give us an example of how to live. What would you say?

Mark's Gospel doesn't give any of those as the reason Jesus came. According to Mark, the reason Jesus came was to rescue rebels.

1. JESUS CAME TO RESCUE REBELS

- Please open your Bibles to Mark chapter 2, verses 13–17.

Read aloud Mark 2:13–17.

- Here are two groups of people – the good guys and the bad guys. The bad guys are made up of people like Levi. Tax collectors in those days were even more hated than they are now. Not only were they seen as cheating their fellow Jews out of their hard-earned cash, but they were also seen as betraying God's people because they were working for the Romans.

- The good guys are the top religious figures of the day – the teachers of the law and the Pharisees. They appeared to be whiter than white, always doing the right thing.
- The question is, who would you expect Jesus to hang around with? Instinctively, we'd expect him to want to be with the good guys, wouldn't we?
- But this is what Jesus says to them: "It is not the healthy who need a doctor, but the sick. I have not come to call the righteous, but sinners." So Jesus is saying here: "I've come for sinners. I've come for people who realize they are living as rebels in God's world." That's what a sinner is – someone who will not let God be God, even though they are living in God's world.
- Jesus makes it quite clear that he is here for people who realize they are bad, not people who think they are good.
- The assumption that Jesus is making here is that all of us are bad, all of us are sinners. But, like these religious people we have just read about, many of us don't think we are sinners.

2. WE ARE ALL REBELS

Use the following illustration: Imagine for a moment that this DVD *[hold up a blank DVD disc]* has on it a complete record of your life. Every day has been recorded. It is a complete and true account not only of everything you've ever said and done, but also of everything you've ever thought. Even your deepest secrets are recorded. Now, imagine that this DVD has been freely distributed to your classmates, your family, in fact everyone you've ever come into contact with. It is even on the shelves at your local supermarket. Now there will be bits on here that you feel quite proud of. Bits you'd want people to watch again and again. But there would also be bits you wouldn't want anyone to see. Maybe it's something no-one knows – not even your closest friend. If my life was on this DVD, it would be a nightmare. I wouldn't be able to stay in the same room as you, I'd be so ashamed. Would you – if you're being honest?

- So why are we like this? Jesus gives us the answer in Mark chapter 7 and we'll read from verse 18.

Read aloud Mark 7:18–23. Explain as you read that the word "unclean" means "unacceptable to God."

- The problem, says Jesus in verse 21, is our hearts. That's what makes us unclean. If we were to trace all of the evil in the world back to its source, the place we'd end up is the human heart.
- "But," you may be saying to yourself, "I'm not that bad. I know I'm not perfect, but I'm not as bad as that." Well, let's turn to Mark chapter 12 and we'll read verses 28–30; remember we looked at these verses earlier.

➲ *Read aloud Mark 12:28–30.*

- Since God made us, and keeps us alive, and gives us every good thing we enjoy, and since he has power and authority over our lives, how should we respond to him? Jesus tells us in verse 30: our response should be to love him.
- The really scary word here is "all" – love God with all your heart, soul, mind and strength. He should have all of everything from us. But actually he's had all of nothing.
- *We* decide exactly what we will do with our heart, soul, mind and strength. We give our hearts to lots of things, but not to our Creator. We don't even know his commands, let alone seek to obey them. We develop relationships with others, but we neglect the main relationship that we were made to have. And instead of loving God, we live as if we *were* God.
- If you think about everything on that DVD – the complete record of your life – it's true isn't it? Each and every one of us rebels against our loving Creator. That rebellion is what the Bible calls "sin."

➲ *You may want to use the following illustration (or come up with another illustration that is particularly relevant to your group):* You'll remember the story of the Titanic. Most of the passengers had no clue how serious their situation was. They were having the party of their lives. But the shipbuilder who designed the boat knew the truth. He knew that the ship would sink and that there weren't enough lifeboats. He knew the situation was deadly serious, so he warned people.

- And Jesus warns us that the situation is deadly serious because of our sin. He spells this out very clearly in Mark chapter 9. Let's look at it from verse 43.

3. WE ARE IN DANGER

▶ *Read aloud Mark 9:43–47.*

- Jesus warns us here that our sin will lead us to hell. If we reject God, then ultimately he will respect that decision – and reject us.
- This isn't easy to talk about. I've got family members who don't realize how serious sin is, so it's really hard for me to say. But I hope you can see that the reason Jesus warns us about hell is because he loves us and doesn't want us to go there.
- He describes hell as a place where the fire never dies out and where there's no rest from punishment. According to Jesus, we should do anything we can to avoid going there. If our foot causes us to sin, we should cut it off. If it's our eye, we should cut it out.
- But as we've seen, our biggest problem is not our foot or our eye, it's our heart. If our problem was the foot, or the hand, we could cut it off. But we can't cut out our heart. So what can we do?

CONCLUSION

▶ *You may want to use the following illustration:* When there is something wrong with us, we need to go to the right person to make sure we treat it properly. Let's imagine I hurt myself on a trampoline and I can't move my arm *[feel free to substitute a more ridiculous injury that no-one could imagine you sustaining]*. Let's ask [one of the group] what is wrong; do you think he / she would know? Let's say I went to the guy at the supermarket who is stacking shelves or a leading academic at the university philosophy department, do you think they'd know? Who would I need to go to to find out what's wrong with my arm? I would need to go to a doctor because he's the one who understands the problem and knows what to do about it.

That's why Jesus came. As he said himself, "It is not the healthy who need a doctor, but the sick. I have not come to call the righteous, but sinners."

He understands the problem and he knows what to do about it. He came to rescue us. And next week, we'll see exactly how Jesus does that.

▶ *Sit with your group and work through TALKBACK.*

OUTLINE OF TALK 4
WHY JESUS DIED

You can use the **Christianity Explored** *DVD Series programme 4 for this week, or use the outline below to develop your own talk. Encourage people to write notes on the UPLOAD page in their* User Guide.

AIM

- To explain that Jesus' death was no accident – it was planned.
- To explain that Jesus died to rescue us from the terrible danger we are in because of our sin.
- To show that Jesus' death makes it possible for us to have a relationship with God.
- To explore the different reactions people have to Jesus' death.

OPENING

Christians are weird people aren't they? Christians celebrate the death of Jesus. Think about that. It's quite a weird thing to do. No other religion celebrates the death of its leader. But for Christians the death of Jesus Christ is massively important.

Why is that? We get the answer in Mark chapter 10, verse 45, where Jesus tells us this:

Read aloud Mark 10:45. Explain as you read that "Son of Man" is Jesus' way of referring to himself.

Jesus says he died "as a ransom for many." Jesus' death is something worth celebrating because it's the only way we can be saved from our sin. It is the way Jesus rescues us. To understand exactly how Jesus rescues us, we need to read an account of Jesus' death, so let's look at Mark chapter 15, starting at verse 22.

Read aloud Mark 15:22–39.

1. GOD WAS ANGRY

- Let's start by looking at verse 33: "At the sixth hour darkness came over the whole land until the ninth hour." Why was there darkness for three whole hours? Some people say this was an eclipse, but there are two problems with that. Passover was always held when it was a full moon and a solar eclipse is impossible during a full moon. And the other thing is that eclipses never last more than about six minutes. This darkness lasted three hours! So something supernatural was going on.
- All the way through the Bible, darkness is a sign of God's judgement and anger.
- Now, sometimes when we get angry it's just because we've got a quick temper. God's anger is not like that. It is his settled, controlled, personal hostility to all that is wrong.

➡ *You may want to use the following illustration (or come up with another illustration that is particularly relevant to your group):* Let's imagine that [use a leader's name] is a serial killer. If God did not punish sin and [the leader] was not caught for the murders, he would get away with it. It would just be wrong, wouldn't it? And it would be awful for the families of all the victims that justice hadn't been done. But because God does punish sin, [the leader] wouldn't get away with it because there is a day when God will judge what he's done wrong. So for God to be consistent and completely fair, he has to deal with sin.

- As we saw last week, it's not only murderers who are sinners. According to Jesus, we're all sinners because none of us has loved God – or other people – as we should. So when darkness falls at the cross, we know that God is acting in judgement to punish sin. But the question is: whose sin is God punishing? Look at verse 34.

2. JESUS WAS ABANDONED

➡ *Read aloud Mark 15:34.*

- On the cross, Jesus was abandoned by God. It was Jesus that God was punishing. But Jesus had led a sinless life. Not even his fiercest enemies could prove he'd done anything wrong. So why would God be punishing him? And why did Jesus willingly subject himself to this?

- Answer: he was willingly taking the punishment for *our* sin. He was punished in *our* place, so that *we* can be rescued.
- And it's not as if Jesus is some innocent third party, being picked on by God. As Paul says in Colossians chapter 1 verse 19, "God was pleased to have all his fulness dwell in him [Jesus]." In other words, Jesus is God. The remarkable truth is that God is making peace with us by willingly sacrificing himself.

➢ *Use the following illustration:* Remember the DVD from last week? *[Hold a blank DVD disc in your right hand.]* Everything that we've ever done, said and thought is on here. And not just the way we've treated others, but the way we've treated God is also recorded.

Now let's suppose that my left hand represents me. *[Hold out your left hand, palm upturned.]* And the ceiling represents God. The Bible says that between us and God is our sin and it separates us from God. *[Place the DVD on the upturned palm of your left hand.]* In fact, the Bible says that God is so perfect, that even if only one second of my life were recorded on this DVD, it would be enough to separate me from God. My sin cuts me off from God.

But let me show you what happened at the cross. *[Hold out your right hand, palm upturned. Your left hand should still have the DVD on it.]* Suppose that my right hand represents Jesus, and remember that the ceiling represents God. As Jesus hung on the cross, there was no barrier between him and God. He always perfectly obeyed God. But, while Jesus was on the cross, he took my sin. *[Now transfer the DVD from the left hand to the right, upturned hand.]*

That's why Jesus cried out, "My God, my God, why have you forsaken me?" as he hung on the cross. It couldn't have been *his* sin that made him feel separated from God, because the Bible tells us that Jesus had led a perfect life. No, it was *our* sin that separated him from God. In those agonising moments, Jesus was taking upon himself all the punishment that our sin, everything on this DVD, deserves.

Jesus died as my substitute, in my place, taking the punishment I deserve. *[Refer people back to your left hand, now empty, with your palm upturned.]* The result of Jesus' extraordinary self-sacrifice is simply this: we can be accepted by God. Jesus paid the price for sin so that we never have to. The amazing truth is that Jesus loved me enough to die for *my* sin. He died for *my* sin, *and* for the sin of *everyone* who puts their trust in him.

3. WE CAN BE ACCEPTED

- Let's look again at verses 37 and 38.

▶ *Read aloud Mark 15:37–38.*

- Here Mark records the exact moment of Jesus' death, but then turns our attention to something that happened at the same moment in the temple, which was on the other side of the city. He wants us to see that the two events are connected.
- When Jesus died, the thirty-foot high curtain in the temple, which was as thick as the span of a man's hand, was torn from top to bottom. This thick curtain used to hang in the temple, dividing the people from the place where God was said to live. The curtain was like a big "Do Not Enter" sign. It said loudly and clearly that it is impossible for sinful people like you and me to walk into God's presence.
- Then suddenly, as Jesus dies on the cross, God rips this curtain in two, from top to bottom. It's as if God is saying: "The way is now open for people to approach me." And that's only possible because Jesus has just paid the price for our sin.

4. REACTIONS TO JESUS' DEATH

- Now there were a lot of different people watching Jesus die. I want you guys to point out for me some of the different reactions people had to the cross.
- So could you look in your Bibles at Mark chapter 15, verse 24 and tell me who "they" are, and what is their reaction to the cross?

▶ *Get answers from the floor.*

- **The soldiers** are busy dividing up his clothes. The most important thing for them is their material possessions and they are so busy chasing after them that they don't realize how important the cross is for them.
- And what about in verses 31–32? Who is reacting to the cross and what is their reaction?

▶ *Get answers from the floor.*

- **The religious leaders** are mocking him. They are so proud and self-satisfied that they don't want to know about Jesus because they think they're okay. They think they don't need him and they're trying to get to God their own way, by their own rules.

➔ *You may want to use the following illustration (or come up with another illustration that is particularly relevant to your group):* It doesn't work, and this is why it doesn't work. Let's imagine that I'm playing a game of football [i.e. soccer]. The football comes towards me and I want to score a goal, so I pick up the ball and by cleverly charging and avoiding my friends as they dive towards me to tackle me, I throw the ball into the net. Now have I scored a legitimate goal? Why is that wrong? Well, I was playing by my own rules and not the referee's rules.

- Those religious leaders believed they could get to God their own way – not God's way, which is through Jesus – so they mocked Jesus and wanted nothing to do with him.
- We see another man's reaction in verse 36 – what's he hoping to see?

➔ *Get answers from the floor.*

- **The man** wants to see a miracle. This bystander wants Elijah to come back from the dead and take Jesus down from the cross. He's there for the show and completely misses the point of the cross. Sometimes all people want is to see miracles or to be entertained. They just want a superficial experience and nothing more.
- What about Mark chapter 15, verse 15? Who's reacting and how?

➔ *Get answers from the floor.*

- **Pilate** is a crowd-pleaser: giving in to peer pressure, giving in to what the crowd is telling him to do. He cares most about his image, his reputation, his popularity. And so he hands over an innocent man to be killed. What about you? Do you care more about your image and popularity, and will that stop you reacting to Jesus in the right way?
- What about Mark chapter 15, verse 39? Who do we see reacting there?

➔ *Get answers from the floor.*

- **The centurion** would have been a hardened professional soldier. He'd seen thousands of people die. But he'd never seen anyone die like this. And his reaction is staggering. He says, "Surely this man was the Son of God!"

CONCLUSION

The right reaction to the cross is to see that Jesus, the Son of God, is giving his life on our behalf. He is dying on the cross so that you and I can be accepted by God – if only we will put our trust in him.

➤ *Sit with your group and work through TALKBACK.*

OUTLINE OF TALK 5
WHY GOD ACCEPTS US

You can use the **Christianity Explored** *DVD Series programme 5 for this week, or use the outline below to develop your own talk. Encourage people to write notes on the UPLOAD page in their* User Guide.

AIM

- To illustrate the fact that most people think God will accept them because of things they have or haven't done.
- To show that God accepts us by grace alone.
- To define grace.

OPENING

This week let me begin by asking you to jot down your answer to the following question: If God asked you, "Why should I give you eternal life?", what would you say?

Just take a couple of minutes now to jot down your answer. Don't worry – you can write down whatever you like because I'm not going to look at them.

Display the question and allow 2 minutes for participants to write down their answers.

Now, if I did look at what you'd written, I reckon we'd find two types of answers.

You will need to have each of the following answers written out in big letters on separate pieces of paper. Hold each of them up as you read them.

The first type of answer is: things you *haven't* done. So maybe you've written something like: "God, you should give me eternal life because... I haven't done anything really bad... I'm not a murderer... I don't steal... I don't lie... I don't swear... I'm not evil, like some of the people you see on TV... I'm not as bad as half the people in my class".

The second type of answer is: things you *have* done. Maybe you've written something like this: "God, you should give me eternal life because... I'm a good person... I try to do what's best... I'm nice to those around me... I go to church... I've been baptized... I pray and read the Bible".

They sound like reasonable answers.

➢ *Rip the papers in two.*

But none of these things are of any use at all when it comes to getting eternal life. Our relationship with God is not based on whether the good things we do outweigh the bad. Any answer which relies upon what I've done or what I haven't done is absolutely useless. Answers that begin "God, you should give me eternal life because ***I***..." will do you no good at all.

Now, there's nothing wrong with those things in themselves. It's good when people try to live honest, selfless lives. But the good things we do won't gain us eternal life. Why? Because they can't solve the problem of our sin.

1. IT'S NOT ABOUT WHAT WE DO

- Remember what Jesus said in Mark chapter 7, verses 20–23?

➢ *Read aloud Mark 7:20–23.*

- The good things we do count for nothing before God, because our key problem lies deep down in our hearts. When Jesus talks about the heart, he's not simply talking about the pump that sends blood around the body. He's referring to the very core of your being – the source of all your urges and instincts, desires and dreams.
- Jesus says we are to "Love the Lord our God with all our heart and with all our soul and with all our mind and with all our strength." But that's not the way we live. So our good deeds, whatever they may be, are fine in themselves – but they're no good at solving the problem that keeps us from God: our sin.
- According to Jesus, our biggest problem is what we are, deep down in our hearts. We are sinful. And nothing we do can change that.

➢ *You may want to use the following illustration (or come up with another illustration that is particularly relevant to your group):* It's like having really bad pimples. They might be so bad that we put Band-Aids [or sticking plasters] on them so that people can't see our horrible pimples. Now those Band-Aids are fine for covering up our problem, but of course they can't actually get rid of the pimples. For that we'd need some industrial strength cream from the doctor. And it's the same with our good deeds. Our good deeds are like those Band-Aids: they might cover up what we're really like inside and make us look better than we really are, but they are powerless to actually cure us.

- But thankfully, that's not the end of the story. There is another answer to God's question, "Why should I give you eternal life?" According to the Bible, the right answer has to do with what God has done.

2. IT'S ALL ABOUT WHAT GOD HAS DONE

- The right answer is something like this: "God, you should let me have eternal life, not because of anything I've done or not done, but because of what Jesus Christ has done." In other words, it's not about the good things we've done for God. It's about the good thing Christ has done for us. He died on the cross so that we could be forgiven our sin. He was abandoned so that we could be accepted.
- Turn with me to Ephesians chapter 2, verse 8 on page ..... of your Bible.

➡ *Read aloud Ephesians 2:8–9.*

- So we are saved by what God has done for us, by God's *grace*. We're not saved by anything we do, by being nice people, or by going to church or reading the Bible. No, we are saved from eternal punishment by Jesus' death on the cross.
- And that's a gift. You can't earn it "by works"; by doing good things. That's why you can't boast about it. "It is the gift of God." The only forgiveness available to us is the forgiveness earned by what Christ did. Because only Christ's death deals with the problem of the human heart.

➡ *Use the following illustration:* It's like the game we played with the spaghetti. [*See page 123 for details of this activity.*] Eventually some of you realized that it just wasn't possible to succeed because the fruit made the spaghetti go all weak and wobbly. Even though we tried to build up a tower, however hard we tried, we couldn't reach the level we were trying to reach. It's the same thing when we try to live up to God's standard because of the good things we've done. We simply can't do it because God is so pure, so perfect, so far beyond our goodness. But the first group that realized they couldn't do it and asked me for help received the chocolate – in fact they got much more than they expected. Why? Because that group realized they'd failed, they were willing to admit it and asked for help. Then they received the gift, and grace is like that.

- Grace is God's gift to us. It's his amazing kindness to us in spite of our rebellion. If we put our trust in Jesus, if we have faith in him, he will accept us, not because of what we've done, but because of what God has done through Jesus. He will accept us not because of how good we are, but because of how good Jesus is.
- But how does God's grace make a difference to us right now?

3. WHAT GRACE DOES FOR US

- If God accepts me because of what Jesus has done, not because of what I have done, then it means God continues to love me, even if I mess up.

▶ *You may want to use the following illustration:* Have you ever been worried that your friends would think badly of you for something? It's horrible isn't it, because you feel you have to cover up the truth about yourself, or your friends won't like you any more. [*Give an example from your own life.*]

- But with God it's completely different. Even though I've done wrong, I can be real with God. He knows what I'm like anyway! I can admit that I've failed and know that he will still love me and accept me. Why? Because of his grace. I don't have to be false like everyone else in the world, wearing a mask, walking around pretending to be something I'm not. With God I can be real because I'm not relating to him through my own performance.

CONCLUSION

Now of course, all this makes Christianity very different from other religions. Every other faith says that if you do this (and don't do that), then God will accept you. But Jesus Christ says that's not true. The only way we can be accepted by God is because of his grace – because he sent Jesus to die on the cross in our place. And remember: it's a free gift. We can't earn it, and we don't deserve it. That's why it's so amazing that God is willing to do this for you and me.

▶ *Sit with your group and work through TALKBACK.*

OUTLINE OF TALK 6
CY JESUS LIVES

You can use the **Christianity Explored** *DVD Series programme 6 for this week, or use the outline below to develop your own talk. Encourage people to write notes on the UPLOAD page in their* User Guide.

AIM

- To explain that Jesus' resurrection is a crucial part of Christianity.
- To investigate the evidence for Jesus' resurrection.
- To explore the consequences of Jesus' resurrection.

OPENING

As we saw in our game earlier it only takes one block to be removed for the whole tower to come crashing down. [*See page 129 for details of this activity.*] The Bible says the same thing about Jesus' resurrection. Listen to this: "if Christ has not been raised, your faith is futile; you are still in your sins" [1 Corinthians 15:17]. So in other words, if Jesus has not risen from the dead, Christianity is a waste of time.

So why is the resurrection so important? It shows us that we can trust Jesus. We can take him at his word. Again and again Jesus had repeatedly and clearly said that he would be killed and three days later rise again. It proves conclusively that Jesus is who he says he is, and it proves that, through faith in him, we can be forgiven and know God.

If the resurrection is that important, we need to make sure it really happened. The first thing we need to be sure about is that Jesus was dead in the first place. We're going to check out some eye-witness evidence to find out if Jesus really did die on the cross.

1. EVIDENCE THAT JESUS DID DIE

- At the end of his account of Jesus's death, Mark focuses on three women who have watched the whole gruesome ordeal. Turn with me to Mark chapter 15 and I'll read to us from verse 40.

▶ *Read aloud Mark 15:40–41.*

- Not only have these women watched Jesus die, but two of them also watch him being buried. Mark writes in verse 47: "Mary Magdalene and Mary the mother of Joses saw where he was laid." They see him die and they watch him being buried. And they are certain he died. Look at chapter 16, verse 1.

▶ *Read aloud Mark 16:1.*

- You wouldn't take spices like that unless you were expecting to find a dead body in the tomb. But it's not only these women who are sure Jesus is dead. Look back at Mark chapter 15, verse 42.

▶ *Read aloud Mark 15:42–45.*

- It was unusual for crucifixion to result in death so quickly, so in verse 44 the Roman governor Pontius Pilate queries the centurion – the same centurion who had stood only a short distance from the cross and watched the extraordinary way in which Jesus had died. The centurion confirms that yes, Jesus was definitely dead. The Romans had many talents, but when it came to killing people, they were experts. So when the centurion said he was dead, he was dead. So Pilate gives Joseph permission to remove the body from the cross.
- Now, let's flip to the evidence in John. He's a writer like Mark who wrote an account of Jesus' life and death. Let me read you what he writes:

▶ *Read aloud John 19:31–34.*

- So the soldiers look at Jesus' body and they see that he is already dead. That's why they don't bother breaking his legs like they do with the other men who are hanging there. This is a bit gruesome, but when the legs were broken it meant that the person could no longer push themselves up and breathe properly. Basically, their own weight suffocated them and they died more quickly. They didn't bother breaking Jesus legs because, like the centurion we just heard about, they were certain that Jesus already was dead.
- Then there are the religious leaders. These guys have always wanted Jesus dead. All the way through Mark they've been plotting to kill him. And now that they have got him where they want him – dead in a tomb – they even make sure that there is no way anyone will be able to steal the body and claim that Jesus had returned from the dead. Here's how they do it. Let me read you from another account of Jesus' life:

➡ *Read aloud Matthew 27:62–66.*

• In other words, Pontius Pilate, the centurion, the Roman soldiers, Joseph, the religious leaders and the women were all absolutely certain that Jesus had died. All the evidence points to the conclusion that Jesus was dead.

2. EVIDENCE THAT JESUS DID RISE

• So we're sure that Jesus died, but can we be sure he rose again? Let's start with the women. Remember that they are on their way to anoint Jesus' body. Let's read from Mark chapter 16, verse 1.

➡ *Read aloud Mark 16:1–8.*

• The huge stone sealing the tomb has been rolled away so they go inside and see a man in a white robe, and Jesus is nowhere to be found. The man in the empty tomb tells them the reason why Jesus' body is not there. Verse 6: "He has risen!"

• Then we read this in John:

➡ *Read aloud John 20:19–20.*

• So Jesus then appears to the disciples and shows them his hands and his side to show that it's really him, he's really alive. And then he appears to Thomas, another disciple. Maybe you can relate to Thomas because he's hard to convince; he doesn't believe the other disciples when they tell him that Jesus has risen from the dead.

➡ *Read aloud John 20:24–25.*

• Now Thomas is a reasonable man. He knows people don't come back from the dead. He says, "Unless I touch the open wounds of his hands and side, I won't believe it."

➡ *You may want to use the following illustration:* Now of course he wouldn't offer to go poking around in someone's open wounds unless he was certain it wasn't going to happen. When you visit sick friends in hospital who have had an operation you don't ask to poke around in their wounds, do you? (If you do, you're sicker than your friend!)

• So Thomas won't believe it. I'll read on:

▶ *Read aloud John 20:26–27.*

- Well, what can Thomas say? The proof of the resurrection is standing right in front of him. Here's what he says in verse 28: "My Lord and my God!"
- Thirty years later, this stubborn, rational, hard-to-convince man was executed because he insisted that Jesus really had done exactly what he said he'd do: he'd risen from the dead. Not only had he seen him with his own eyes, he'd spoken with him, and he'd touched him with his own hands.
- The Gospels alone tell us of eleven separate occasions where Jesus is seen after his death, at different times and in different places, by different people. Another writer in the Bible, Paul, tells us that over 500 people saw Jesus at one time, many of whom were still living when Paul was writing [1 Corinthians 15:6]. So Paul was saying to his readers, "If you don't believe me, go and talk to the eye-witnesses. They're still alive and they'll tell you I'm telling the truth."
- So we're left with a staggering conclusion. Jesus died and was buried. Three days later he rose from the dead and was seen alive by hundreds of people, many of whom were later to be killed for insisting that Jesus really had risen from the dead.

CONCLUSION

The Bible tells us there are two things we should learn from the resurrection. The first is that Jesus got through death so he can get us through it as well. We all die and we can't avoid it, but we have no need to fear death if we trust in Jesus.

The second thing the resurrection proves is that Jesus will be our judge. The Bible says: "[God] has set a day when he will judge the world with justice by the man he has appointed. He has given proof of this to all men by raising [Jesus] from the dead." [Acts 17:31]

Now that's a massive thought. The resurrection proves that Jesus Christ will come again to judge everyone in the world! So our sin *does* matter, it *will* be judged and Jesus will be our judge. But the wonderful thing, as we've seen, is that Jesus can also be our rescuer, if only we will put our trust in him.

▶ *Sit with your group and work through TALKBACK.*

OUTLINE OF CY WE'RE NOT ALONE TALK 1
CY IT'S TOUGH TO FOLLOW JESUS

This talk must be delivered "live" – do not use the Weekend Away programmes from the **Christianity Explored** *DVD Series. Encourage people to write notes on the UPLOAD page in their* User Guide.

AIM

- To show that Jesus warns us to consider seriously what is involved in following him before we do so.
- To explain that anyone who wants to follow Jesus must be willing to suffer and to put him above everything else in their lives.

OPENING

Did you notice that if you made your tower too thin, it was easily knocked down, but harder to hit with the sponges? Fat towers were harder to knock down, but easier to hit. [*See page 136 for details of this activity.*]

You could see the need to plan your tower carefully before you built it, especially as you knew it would come under attack. Jesus talks in a similar way about planning ahead. Turn with me to Luke chapter 14, verse 28 on page ..... of your Bible.

1. COUNTING THE COST OF FOLLOWING JESUS

Read aloud Luke 14:28–30.

- Jesus describes a man building a tower. Before he builds his tower he must stop and think if he really has all the resources and the abilities to complete that tower. Because if he starts building, but only has enough money to lay the foundation, everyone will be pointing at his foundation and laughing at how short-sighted he's been.
- Let's read on.

Read aloud Luke 14:31–32.

- This time, Jesus describes a king going out to war. Before a king goes to war he must stop and think whether or not he can win the battle. If he can't, and he doesn't have the men and resources to do it, then he will try to make peace. To make the wise decision, the king must think first and plan ahead.
- Why does Jesus tell these stories? It's because he wants us to think first about what is involved before we commit to being his disciples. Look with me at verse 27 and 33. Jesus says:

Read aloud Luke 14:27 and then 14:33.

2. THE COST - SUFFERING

- First, in order to be Jesus' disciple we have to "carry our cross". That's what he says in verse 27. What does Jesus mean by that? He doesn't mean we all have to die like he did on a cross. He means that every Christian must face suffering of one kind or another.

You may want to use the following illustration (or come up with another illustration that is particularly relevant to your group): For example, I have friends whose families rejected them when they trusted in Jesus. I know other people whose friends laughed at them and thought they were stupid when they became Christians. And of course, in many countries around the world Christians are actually tortured and killed simply because they are living for Jesus. The Christian life isn't rosy – it can be very hard at times.

At this point, you might want to ask one of the leaders, older participants, or a specially invited guest (e.g. a missionary from your church) to illustrate this truth from their own experience.

3. THE COST - PUTTING JESUS FIRST

- Then in verse 33 Jesus says that people must "give up everything" they have to be his disciples. This means that a follower of Jesus must live for him and not for themselves.
- It means that Jesus has to come first in their decisions, in terms of what they do with their lives, what they do with their spare time, how they treat their parents, who they go out with and so on, because they've recognized that *they* are not number one, but Jesus is number one.

CONCLUSION

Over the last six weeks, we've seen what an amazing person Jesus is. We've seen how courageous and compassionate and kind he is. We've seen that we can trust his words. And we've seen how powerful he is. So actually, it's a fantastic joy to put your trust in him because you know you can trust him with your life.

➲ *Illustrate this briefly from your own life.*

For me, life began when I stopped trusting in myself and started trusting him. So it's wonderful to be a Christian, but it's not always easy. That's why Jesus says what he says here: so that we'll stop and think what the cost will be before putting our trust in him.

➲ *Sit with your group and work through TALKBACK.*

OUTLINE OF CY WE'RE NOT ALONE TALK 2
CY YOU NEED THE HOLY SPIRIT

This talk must be delivered "live" – do not use the Weekend Away programmes from the **Christianity Explored** *DVD Series. Encourage people to write notes on the UPLOAD page in their* User Guide.

AIM

- To explain what Jesus means when he calls the Holy Spirit "Counsellor".
- To describe how the Holy Spirit guides, shows us our sin and gives us the desire to please God.
- To explain that Jesus promises that when we trust in him, he will come and live in us by his Spirit.

OPENING

After what we just heard Jesus saying about carrying our cross and giving up everything for him, some of you are probably wondering how you can possibly live like that. It sounds impossible!

Humanly speaking it is impossible. But in these remaining talks we are going to look at four ways that God makes it possible: the Holy Spirit, the church, the Bible and prayer.

We just saw in the game we played how important it is sometimes to be guided by someone. [*See page 139 for details of this activity.*] Some of you were guided pretty badly and found it doubly difficult! But, if you are a Christian, you have the perfect guide: the Holy Spirit.

Look at what Jesus says about the Holy Spirit in John chapter 14. It's on page ..... of your Bible. I'll read from verse 15.

1. WHO IS THE HOLY SPIRIT?

Read aloud John 14:15–18.

- Jesus' promise is that those who trust him will have a "Counsellor" – in other words, a helper, comforter, guide, instructor – who will live with them and in them.
- Notice that Jesus says "another Counsellor". He is saying that this Counsellor will do for believers what he himself did for them while he was on earth: teaching them, challenging them, enabling them to understand God's word, encouraging them and supporting them.
- So the "Counsellor" who comes to live in Christians is the Spirit of Jesus himself. It's what Christians mean when they talk about "the Holy Spirit".
- By the way, the Spirit described in this passage is not some sort of weird impersonal power, like the Jedi "force". Jesus calls the Holy Spirit "him" and "he".

Ask one of the leaders (or a Christian participant) to talk about how the Holy Spirit has affected their life.

2. THE HOLY SPIRIT SHOWS PEOPLE THEIR SIN

- Now, just as Jesus showed people the sin in their lives, so his Spirit does the same today.
- Do you remember the way that Jesus spoke to the rich young man [Week 5] – gently pointing out his sin and telling him to build "treasure in heaven" instead? Well that's exactly what the Holy Spirit does in people's hearts today. It's an amazing thing as we live the Christian life to be guided in that way by the Holy Spirit.

3. THE HOLY SPIRIT GIVES US THE DESIRE TO OBEY GOD

- None of us naturally has the desire to obey God. You might have realized that from your own experience. That's why we need the Spirit to change us.
- Turn with me to the Old Testament, to the book of Ezekiel, chapter 36 on page ..... of your Bible. This is a promise from God himself, to all those who put their trust in him.

Read aloud Ezekiel 36:26–27.

- So, the Spirit changes people's hearts, giving them the desire to obey God, enabling them to do things that previously would have seemed too hard for them or that they had rebelled against. That longing in your heart to go God's way is a sign that the Holy Spirit is at work in your life, fighting against everything that keeps you from knowing God more fully.

CONCLUSION

Now, you might be thinking, how do we receive the Holy Spirit? Well, the Bible tells us that we receive the Holy Spirit once and for all when we become a Christian [John 14:15–16]. So when we start following Jesus, the Holy Spirit comes to live in us. And that's one of the reasons why, when you become a Christian, you're never alone.

▶ *Sit with your group and work through TALKBACK.*

OUTLINE OF CY WE'RE NOT ALONE TALK 3
CY THE CHURCH IS YOUR FAMILY

This talk must be delivered "live" – do not use the Weekend Away programmes from the **Christianity Explored** *DVD Series. Encourage people to write notes on the UPLOAD page in their* User Guide.

AIM

- To explain that a church is a family of Christians who meet together.
- To show that we need to help each other if we are to live the Christian life.
- To explain that a good church will teach the Bible truthfully, encourage each other, remember Jesus' death and pray together.

OPENING

What springs to mind when you think of a church? Maybe you think of a building in the centre of your town, or a Sunday service with lots of old ladies wearing hats, or a place where some people go for a coffee morning now and again.

But the Bible says church is none of those things. It's a family of people who believe in Jesus.

1. WHAT IS A CHURCH?

- Look with me at Hebrews chapter 10, verse 25 on page ..... of your Bible. It says: "Let us not give up meeting together, as some are in the habit of doing, but let us encourage one another". So the church is about meeting with one another and encouraging each other.
- One of the amazing things about becoming a Christian is that you are immediately part of a family. The Bible often talks about God as our Father and Christians as his children. So, every Christian has a whole bunch of new brothers and sisters who are looking out for them.

Ask one of the leaders (or a Christian participant) to talk about how the church has been an encouragement to them.

- Proverbs 13:20 says: "he who walks with the wise grows wise, but a companion of fools suffers harm". This verse is talking about how you can spend time with two different types of people. If you hang out with a fool, the Bible says you will suffer harm. If you hang out with a wise person, the Bible says you will grow wise. We need to have Christians around us because they will have a positive influence on us.
- So the Christian life is not a solo activity; it's not about going on your own – it's about teamwork.
- It's like the game we played a moment ago. [*See page 141 for details of this activity.*] Everybody in the church has a role to play, and they need to work together so that the whole church benefits and serves God together.

Give an example from your own life of how being surrounded by like-minded people helps you. For example: When I was growing up, I used to love rowing. I would often row up and down the river in my single boat trying hard to get faster and row better. Every now and again I would do a time trial, which I found incredibly hard because there was no-one alongside to help me. But when there were other boats alongside me trying to get their times better, it encouraged me to row harder because I could see them working hard at it as well.

2. WHAT HAPPENS AT CHURCH?

- So what's church supposed to be like? There's a book in the Bible called Acts and it's like a time capsule because it shows what the very first churches were like. Turn with me to Acts chapter 2, verse 42 on page ..... of your Bible. It tells us that the church "devoted themselves to the apostles' teaching and to the fellowship, to the breaking of bread and to prayer."
- What four things happen here? [*Ask them to shout out.*] They hear the Bible taught truthfully, they care for one another, they remember Jesus' death by breaking bread and they pray.
- It's so important to find a church where all these things happen.

CONCLUSION

Church should be about people who follow Jesus spending time with one another, encouraging one another and getting to know God better.

Sit with your group and work through TALKBACK.

OUTLINE OF CY WE'RE NOT ALONE TALK 4
CY IT'S GOOD TO TALK

This talk must be delivered "live" – do not use the Weekend Away programmes from the **Christianity Explored** *DVD Series. Encourage people to write notes on the UPLOAD page in their* User Guide.

AIM

- To show that the Bible and prayer are vital to the Christian life.
- To explain that when we read the Bible God talks to us.
- To explain that when we pray we talk to God.

OPENING

You may want to use the following illustration (or come up with another illustration that is particularly relevant to your group): Good communication is important, isn't it? Some people really aren't very good at it. I saw a sign in an office which said: "Would the person who took the step ladder yesterday please bring it back or further steps will be taken".

Well, good communication is the key to knowing God. We need to speak regularly and honestly with God, and also listen to what he has to say to us. That's why Christians pray and read the Bible – in the Bible God talks to us and in prayer we talk to God.

1. GOD TALKS TO US

You may want to use the following illustration (or come up with another illustration that is particularly relevant to your group): Imagine the postman delivers a letter to you. You pick it up, open the envelope and then, if you're anything like me, you look at the bottom of the letter to see who it's from. Because when we know who it's written by, it affects the way we read it. If it comes from your friend or is your examination results, you'd read it really carefully. But if it's a letter from your dentist, or someone you've never heard of trying to sell you encyclopedias, you'd probably just look it over quickly and then throw it away. But when we pick up the Bible, we should remember that it's a letter from God. So we'll want to read it really carefully.

• Let's look at Psalm 1 together. It's on page ..... of your Bible.

Read aloud Psalm 1:1–3.

• So verse 2 tells us that the Christian's "delight is in the law of the LORD, and on his law he meditates day and night." So Christians are to take their lead not from the people around them, but from God's law, the Bible. When we read the Bible, we are reading God's words to us. God talks to us.

• And as we listen, we become, verse 3 says, "like a tree planted by streams of water, which yields its fruit in season and whose leaf does not wither." It's like one of those great big trees you sometimes see in the forest – it's so big, you can't get your arms around it – it's been there for years. Storms have come and gone but it's still there. And it's still producing fruit, year in year out. Amazing that it keeps going. But of course, it wouldn't keep going if it had no water. Trees need it to survive.

• And that's what it says here: if we want to be strong and keep going year after year, we need the Bible – just as a tree needs water.

• Let's read on.

Read aloud Psalm 1:4–6.

• Did you notice the contrast there? These people, who don't care what God has to say to them, are like "chaff". That's the useless bits that are left over at harvest time when the farmer is collecting grain. You know, the husks and bits of straw. And, unlike the tree by the river, they just get blown away by the wind.

• It's amazing to know that God "watches over" those who have put their trust in him. But there's a warning that people who ignore the words of the One who made them have no future and will perish. So, will we be like chaff, without roots, with no stability and no future? Or will we be like the tree, firmly rooted and fed and strengthened by what we read in the Bible?

2. WE TALK TO GOD

• It's really hard to communicate with people without words, isn't it? Some of you were better at it than others when we played the game, but words just make it so much easier, don't they? [*See page 144 for details of this activity.*] It's the same if we want to build a relationship with God. We're going to need to talk to him – and that's what prayer is all about.

- Why don't we look together at one of the prayers in the Bible? Look at Acts chapter 4, verse 23, on page ..... of your Bible.

▶ *Read aloud Acts 4:23–31.*

- Can you think of the worst time in your life, when everything seemed to be going horribly wrong? Well, that is exactly where the disciples are at this point. Their two main spokesmen have just been interrogated by the highest religious authorities who are determined to shut them up. So what's the answer? What's the best thing to do in this situation? Answer: they pray together.

- And look at who they pray to in verse 24: the "Sovereign Lord... [who] made the heaven and the earth and the sea, and everything in them." It's as if they're saying, "Lord, you made the universe, our world and all the people who live in it, and you're in control of everything, even those people who are threatening us."

- That's who Christians pray to: a God who is unimaginably powerful. However much people try, plotting against this "Sovereign Lord" is a complete waste of time. So even though Herod, Pilate, the Gentiles and the people of Israel all conspired to have Jesus killed, verse 28 tells us: "They did what your power and will had decided beforehand should happen." You have to be unimaginably powerful to have your enemies do what *you* want, even as they are doing what *they* want!

- The disciples then ask for God's help. They pray in verse 29, "Now, Lord, consider their threats and enable your servants to speak your word with great boldness." And God responds to their prayer in a very visible way: "After they prayed, the place where they were meeting was shaken. And they were all filled with the Holy Spirit and spoke the word of God boldly." By speaking the word of God boldly, they are doing exactly what the authorities have forbidden them to do. You wouldn't do that unless you believed that God was in control!

- Of course, God doesn't always answer prayer in the way Christians want or expect. At moments like that, we must remember that God is still in control; that he has a plan; that he is wiser and more loving than we are; and that the decisions he makes are trustworthy. There will be difficult situations that we won't understand until we're with God in eternity.

- So when Christians pray, they are praying to the Sovereign Lord, who is in complete control of everything that will happen. It's an amazing privilege. And it means that Christians can talk to God about anything. He is interested in even the small details of their lives.
- When talking to God, you mustn't forget to say the things you'd say to a trusted friend. You'd apologize for the things you've done wrong and ask them to forgive you. You'd thank them, ask them for help (for yourself or for other people), tell them your secrets, pour out your heart to them. The difference is, when you talk to God, you're talking to someone who is in control of everything – and who loves to give you every good thing you need.

CONCLUSION

What is your attitude to prayer and the Bible? Sometimes people use them as a last resort when everything else fails. There they are on the way to school and they've got a really tough exam coming up; they haven't done much studying, so they pray. Something like this: "Please God, get me through this test and I promise I'll be nice to grandma from now on." And sometimes we treat the Bible in the same way. It's where you go for some emotional encouragement in case of emergencies.

But praying and reading the Bible shouldn't be like a big red button we press only in case of emergency. Actually, it's what Christians do every day because they want to know God better.

> *Ask one of the leaders (or a Christian participant) to talk about the importance of speaking to God and God speaking to them through his word.*

> *Sit with your group and work through TALKBACK.*

OUTLINE OF TALK 7
CY WE SHOULD BELIEVE

You can use the **Christianity Explored** *DVD Series programme 7 for this week, or use the outline below to develop your own talk. Encourage people to write notes on the UPLOAD page in their* User Guide.

AIM

- To remind people who Jesus is.
- To remind people that Jesus came to die.
- To explain that a Christian "must deny himself and take up his cross and follow [Jesus]" (Mark 8:34).

OPENING

I want to look finally at Mark chapter 8 in order to discover exactly what it means to be a Christian. In this chapter, we see Jesus explaining that a Christian is someone who knows who Jesus is, understands why he came, and is prepared to follow him – whatever the cost.

So first, who is Jesus?

1. WHO IS JESUS?

- Do you remember Mark told us the answer in the very first sentence of his book. He said that Jesus Christ is "the Son of God." But of course, for ages, Jesus' own followers couldn't see that.
- Jesus, for his part, forces them to ask questions about who he is by doing amazing things – as we've seen. They watch him calming a violent storm, curing incurable illness, bringing a little girl back from the dead. They even hear him claiming to be able to forgive sin. And yet they don't come up with the obvious answer: that this really is God's Son, the Christ, the one who'd been promised throughout the Old Testament. They were expecting it, were desperately hoping for it, but now that he's there, standing right in front of them, they just don't see it.

Display the picture shown here. (It can be downloaded from the website at www.christianityexplored.com). Have you ever seen one of those trick pictures that seem to show one thing but – looked at another way – show something entirely different? The most well-known one is probably this picture of a beautiful young woman. Despite staring at that picture for a long time, it was ages before I could see the beautiful young woman. All I could see was a hideous old hag. And if you're an amateur psychologist, I'm sure you could have some fun with that fact!

- In a similar way, when you look at Jesus you see a man but you also see God. The two are obvious, they are there for all to see, but even though the disciples stared and stared for several years, all they could see was the man.
- But then something changed. Look with me at Mark chapter 8, verse 27.

Read aloud Mark 8:27–29.

- This is a big step forward for the disciples. Finally, they've recognized that Jesus is the Christ, the King promised in the Old Testament, who would have the power and authority of God himself.
- Jesus asks them a scorching question here: "Who do you say I am?" It's very personal. And at this point in Mark's Gospel, it also gets very personal for us. Who do *we* say Jesus is? What do *we* see as we look at the face of Jesus? Can we only see a man or can we also see that Jesus is God?
- So the disciples have seen who Jesus is. But do they understand why Jesus came?

2. WHY DID JESUS COME?

- Look at verse 31.

Read aloud Mark 8:31–32.

- That's why Jesus came. He came to die. In fact, it's *necessary* that he die. It's the only way in which sinful people like you and I can be brought back into a relationship with God.
- But Peter has this image of Jesus as king so clearly in his mind that it just seems wrong to him that Jesus would have to die. And he tells Jesus so. How on earth can a king set up his kingdom by dying? That's ridiculous. But Jesus tells Peter that he's got it all wrong. Look at verse 33.

➲ *Read aloud Mark 8:33.*

- In a way, I don't blame Peter for thinking like this. After all, there are two ways of looking at the cross. If, as Jesus says, we have in mind "the things of men," there is tremendous weakness at the cross. Jesus seems exposed, humiliated, and defeated. From the human point of view, the cross seems to prove that Jesus had got it all wrong. He was right about so many things, but if he really *was* the Son of God, why couldn't he come down from the cross? A king should be on a throne, not a cross.
- But what do we see if we look at the cross from another angle – from God's point of view? What if we have in our minds, as Jesus says, "the things of God"? Then we can see the cross as part of God's rescue plan. We can see that Jesus chose to be separated from God so that we don't have to be, paying the terrible price for our sin, being executed in our place. From God's point of view, and from ours if we have in mind the things of God, this is not weakness. In fact, there has never been a more powerful moment in history.

➲ *You may want to use the following illustration (or come up with another illustration that is particularly relevant to your group):* On 13 January 1982, millions of television viewers watched as a balding, middle-aged man swam in the icy cold water of a river in Washington DC. Seven inches of snow had fallen that day. The water was so cold that life expectancy was no more than a few minutes. A helicopter quickly reached the scene, and let down a rope to haul the man to safety. The viewers at home were amazed as the man twice grabbed hold of the rope, then quite deliberately let it go. Each time the rope was lowered to him, he had a chance of survival, but he chose to let it go. And – in front of millions of avidly watching viewers – the man eventually died. It seems like a futile and pointless death. But we need to see the bigger picture.

Five minutes earlier, a Boeing 737 jetliner carrying eighty-three passengers and crew had departed from National Airport's main runway. However, ice had built up on the wings as it waited for take-off, so it couldn't get high enough off the ground. It hit a bridge heavy with commuters and then plunged nose-first into the frozen Potomac River. The survivors struggled in the freezing river amid ice chunks, debris, luggage, seat cushions and jet fuel. Thankfully, a rescue helicopter arrived and let down its rope. The television cameras then picked out a balding, middle-aged man. He grabbed the rope, and deliberately gave it to somebody else, who was then pulled to safety. The man did this twice before – exhausted – he drowned.

- When we have all the details in front of us, an apparently futile death is shown to be purposeful, courageous and amazingly loving.
- And Jesus' death is all of those things. He died as part of a rescue mission. In his amazing love he came to earth and died in our place, taking the punishment that we deserved, so that we could enter into a relationship with God. He was forsaken so that we need never be.
- There are two ways of seeing the cross. We can see it from a human point of view, as a pathetic and needless death. Or we can see it from God's point of view, as our only means of rescue. Our lives, as well as our deaths, will be determined by the way in which we respond to what Jesus did on the cross.
- And that leads us to one last question: what does Jesus demand? Because it is not enough to recognize who Jesus is, or even why he came: just like the disciples, we also need to understand what it means to follow him.
- Look at Mark chapter 8 verse 34.

3. WHAT DOES JESUS DEMAND?

Read aloud Mark 8:34.

- First of all, Jesus tells us to deny ourselves. That means not living as if we are the centre of the universe. It means no longer living for ourselves but for God and for others.

➢ *You may want to use the following illustration (or come up with another illustration that is particularly relevant to your group):* You'll have many choices in your life over the next couple of years. Chances are you'll be choosing what job you want to do, whether you'll go to university, where you want to live, who you want to marry, whether you'll have kids. And those are all good things, but are we prepared to put Jesus before all of them?

- But Jesus' call goes further than that, as you can see from verse 34. He says we must also "take up our cross". So this is Jesus' offer to his hearers: "I will die for you, but you must be prepared to die for me, if you want to follow me." It's a call to come and die to our old way of life.

➢ *You may want to use the following illustration (or come up with another illustration that is particularly relevant to your group):* In the early years of the twentieth century, the explorer Ernest Shackleton put an advertisement in London newspapers to try and find men who would come with him on his polar expedition. The advertisement ran like this: "Men wanted for a hazardous journey. Small wages, bitter cold, long months in complete darkness, constant danger, safe return doubtful." Needless to say, not many people applied.

- But Jesus says a similar thing to us: "take up your cross". Of course, Jesus isn't saying that everyone who follows him will face a violent death. But, if you do decide to follow him, you will face suffering at least. That's because friends, family, and those around you may find what you believe and the way you live uncomfortable or even offensive. And that can be really tough.
- So, a Christian is not only someone who sees clearly who Jesus is and why he came. A Christian is someone who is prepared to follow him, whatever the cost.
- Well, surely there's too much at stake here. By following Jesus, there is simply too much to lose. The price seems too high. Jesus knows this, and goes on to give us a great reason to follow him, no matter what the cost. Look with me at the next couple of verses.

➢ *Read aloud Mark 8:35–37.*

4. WHY LIVE FOR JESUS?

- It's a great reason to follow Jesus. Jesus promises us that if we give our lives – our souls – to him then he will save them. We will have an amazing relationship with God now and an amazing eternity with him when we die. What good will it be to us if we gain everything the world has to offer – popularity, money, fame – but then lose the most valuable thing we have: our souls?
- Jesus will judge the world, whether we like it or not. And we can choose whether or not the judge will also be our rescuer. And ultimately, we will be treated very fairly. We will be treated by Jesus in exactly the same way as we have treated him, as he tells us in Mark chapter 8, verse 38.

Read aloud Mark 8:38.

- Because Jesus is the one who will judge the world, it's a no-brainer to entrust him with my life, my energy, my love. In doing that, I know that those things will be saved. And actually, whatever we might lose by following Christ is nothing compared to what we will gain – not only in this life but also in the life to come.
- Jesus tells us to give up the very things that will destroy us – self-love, self-worship, self-will – and exchange them for eternal life.
- So what will you do? Think about it very carefully, for there will be a day when Christ returns and he will treat us in the same way we have treated him.

CONCLUSION

In 1000 AD, 186 years after he died, people opened the tomb of the Emperor Charlemagne, who used to be one of the most powerful men alive. As they pushed back the spider webs, they saw an extraordinary thing. In the middle of all the finery buried with him – the gold, the jewels, the priceless treasure – there was the skeleton of Charlemagne himself, still seated on his throne, still wearing his crown. In his lap, there lay a Bible, and a bony finger rested on Mark chapter 8, verse 36: "What good is it for a man to gain the whole world, yet forfeit his soul?"

I wonder what answer the king gave?

Sit with your group and work through TALKBACK.

SETTING UP THE COURSE
ORGANIZING THE WEEKEND OR DAY AWAY

Jesus urged people to count the cost of following him before making a decision to do so. In the same way, your group needs to have a clear understanding of what the Christian life involves before committing to it. With this in mind, the "***CY*** We're Not Alone" weekend or day away has been placed before Week 7 – the final week – when participants are invited to repent and believe.

The material covered during this time aims to paint a realistic picture of what the Christian life is like, and to reassure people that they will not be alone if they choose to begin following Christ. Participants are given the chance to count the cost and are assured that God will graciously provide his Holy Spirit, the church family, the Bible and prayer to uphold them.

In Week 4, you should let participants know that there will be a weekend or day away. Give a brief idea of what will happen, and let them know that they will need their parents' permission to attend.

In Week 5 hand out invitations and in Week 6 hand out schedules for the weekend or day away.

Ensure that your prayer team has been notified and that they are praying ahead.

The weekend or day away allows plenty of time for leaders to continue to build trusting relationships with participants. Use the free time for activities that will facilitate this (for example, playing a team sport).

Testimonies from members of the youth group are also important, because they give participants an insight into the practicalities of Christian living. Choose some of your youth group to present their testimonies and help them to prepare what they will say. Testimonies can be presented at any point during the weekend or day away.

During the weekend or day away, there should be no singing, praying or anything that could make participants feel unduly pressured or uncomfortable.

EXAMPLE SCHEDULE FOR WEEKEND AWAY

FRIDAY	
Arrive	7:00 p.m.
Welcome followed by organized activities	7:30 p.m.
SATURDAY	
Leaders' prayer meeting	8:30 a.m.
Breakfast	9:00 a.m.
Talk 1 – *CY* It's Tough to Follow Jesus followed by TALKBACK	10:00 a.m.
Break	11:00 a.m.
Talk 2 – *CY* You Need the Holy Spirit followed by TALKBACK	11:30 a.m.
Lunch	12:30 p.m.
Free afternoon / Organized activities	1:30 p.m.
Dinner	6:30 p.m.
Talk 3 – *CY* The Church is Your Family followed by TALKBACK	7:30 p.m.
Free evening / Organized activities	8:30 p.m.
SUNDAY	
Leaders' prayer meeting	8:30 a.m.
Breakfast	9:00 a.m.
Attend church with your group if possible	10:00 a.m.
Lunch	12:00 p.m.
Talk 4 – *CY* It's Good to Talk followed by TALKBACK	1:00 p.m.
Leave	2:00 p.m.

EXAMPLE SCHEDULE FOR DAY AWAY

Arrive	10:00 a.m.
Welcome	10:30 a.m.
Talk 1 – *CY* It's Tough to Follow Jesus followed by TALKBACK	11:00 a.m.
Break	12:00 p.m.
Talk 2 – *CY* You Need the Holy Spirit followed by TALKBACK	12:30 p.m.
Lunch	1:30 p.m.
Free time / Organized activities	2:30 p.m.
Talk 3 – *CY* The Church is Your Family followed by TALKBACK	4:30 p.m.
Break	5:30 p.m.
Talk 4 – *CY* It's Good to Talk followed by TALKBACK	6:00 p.m.
Leave	7:00 p.m.

SETTING UP THE COURSE
GETTING FEEDBACK

Feedback forms, given out during the last week of the course, are a great way to challenge participants to think about what they have learned, and to help leaders plan a way forward once the course is ended. An example feedback form is shown below and a printer-friendly version can be downloaded from www.christianityexplored.com/cy

Name

1 **Before you began *CY*, how would you have described yourself?**

- ☐ I didn't believe in God
- ☐ I wasn't sure if God existed or not
- ☐ I believed in God but not in Jesus Christ
- ☐ A Christian
- ☐ Something else ______________________

2 **Now that you've finished *CY*, how would you describe yourself?**

- ☐ I understand who Jesus is, why he came and what it means to follow him. I have put my trust in him.
- ☐ I wouldn't call myself a Christian, but I would like to find out more.
- ☐ Other ______________________

3 **If you have not yet put your trust in Jesus, what is stopping you?**

4 **What would you like to do now?**

- ☐ I am interested in joining a follow-up course (a course that will help me to continue in the Christian life).
- ☐ I'd like to read the ***Christianity Explored*** book to help me remember what I discovered on ***CY***.
- ☐ I don't want to do anything more at this stage.
- ☐ I would like to join a church.
- ☐ I am happy at the church I go to.

5 **On a scale of 1 to 10 how much did you enjoy *CY*?**
(1 = I really hated it; 10 = I really loved it.)

6 **Anything else you'd like to tell us?**

This section is intended for every leader, and will prepare you to lead participants through the course. We would strongly urge you to work through this section - and meet with your fellow leaders to discuss it - before ***CY*** begins. It's impossible to be over-prepared for the course!

SECTION 2
TRAINING NOTES

> *Read through this section, completing the exercises as you go.*

> *Before the course begins, set aside a few hours when you and your co-leaders can meet for a meal, to pray together, get to know one another and discuss any practical issues that may have arisen from reading this section.*

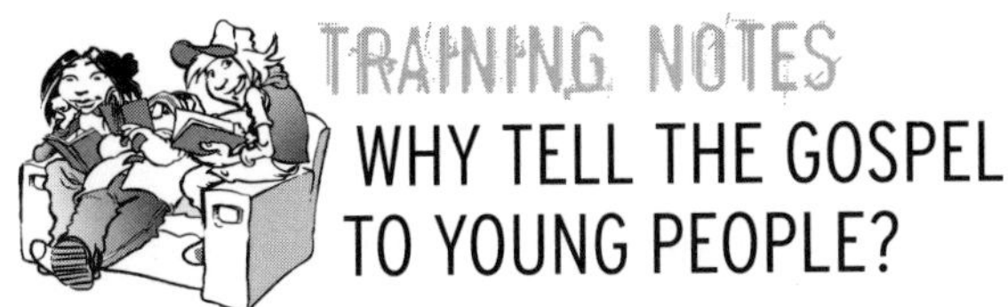

TRAINING NOTES

WHY TELL THE GOSPEL TO YOUNG PEOPLE?

Why would anyone want to run a course on Mark's Gospel with a group of young people?

We all know that youth work is hard. There are heartaches, disappointments and difficulties. Surely it would be better to provide games and entertainment for young people and then try to reach them when they are older?

By that time, of course, if entertainment is all we've offered them, they will have long since found better entertainment elsewhere. It is, after all, something the world specializes in!

But as Christians, we can offer our young people something much more profound and compelling than entertainment, something that the world cannot compete with. We can offer the gospel.

And when the gospel is presented in all its fulness, young lives can be changed by God radically and miraculously – forever. Although reaching young people with the gospel of Jesus Christ and training them to be committed disciples can be hard, it can also be extraordinarily joyful, and it is vital in the eyes of God.

1. GOD DESIRES THAT YOUNG PEOPLE SHOULD KNOW HIM

The writer of Ecclesiastes considers what life is like when every possible pleasure is indulged – but God is excluded. He reaches a simple conclusion: "Remember your Creator in the days of your youth" (Ecclesiastes 12:1). We should be mindful of our Creator when we are young.

Sometimes we view the teenage years of young people as a phase that must be passed through before we can focus on winning them to Christ. Provided they get through those difficult years without getting into too many unhelpful things, and keep coming to church once in a while, we are content. But God wants young people to know him and be in a living relationship with him.

2. THE TIME TO KNOW GOD IS WHEN WE ARE YOUNG

The writer of Ecclesiastes reflects that it is better to know God "before the days of trouble come and the years approach when you will say, 'I find no pleasure in them'" (12:1).

Why is that so? Because knowing God from our youth gives us reason and purpose for the rest of our lives. We live the life we were intended to live. Equally, God does not want us to waste the years he has given us. He wants us to use them for him, taking "pleasure in them" by serving him.

Great leaders are often formed when they are young. King David knew and served God from a young age; Daniel followed God from youth and even Timothy was reminded by Paul that he had been taught about God from his youth.

When God saves a young person, he uses their youth to form them, to mould their character and attitudes, to shape a person who will follow Jesus for the rest of their lives – and influence others to do the same.

Think of what a difference a young person could make living fully for Jesus Christ: their witness at school; all the friends they can reach; the salt and light that they can be in a lost world. The young people of today are the serving, growing Christians of tomorrow and even the leaders of the future. If we invest our lives and energies in young people, we are investing in those who have the potential to love and glorify God for decades to come.

3. IF WE WAIT IT COULD BE TOO LATE

At the end of chapter 12, the writer of Ecclesiastes urges us to remember our Creator "before the silver cord is severed or the golden bowl is broken" (v6) and "the dust returns to the ground it came from, and the spirit returns to God who gave it" (v7).

These are pictures of death. But it is not only the old who die; sometimes the young die too. And ultimately, everyone – whether young or old – will face death and the judgement of God.

So we *must* share the gospel with young people before it is too late.

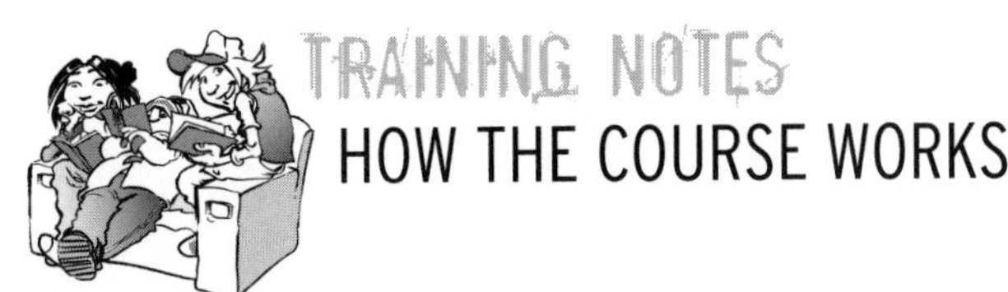

TRAINING NOTES
HOW THE COURSE WORKS

During this seven-week course, as Mark's Gospel is read and taught, you will be helping young people to explore three questions that cut right to the heart of Christianity:

- Who was Jesus?
- Why did Jesus come?
- What does Jesus demand of those who want to follow him?

In other words, the course is all about:

- Jesus' identity
- Jesus' mission
- Jesus' call.

The first six weeks focus on Jesus' identity and mission. In particular, your youth group will explore the problem of sin and the wonder of forgiveness.

There is then a weekend or day away when participants are given the chance to consider the cost of following Christ – and are assured that God will graciously provide his Holy Spirit, the church family, the Bible and prayer to uphold them.

The objective in the final week is to emphasize Christ's call in Mark 8:34: "If anyone would come after me, he must deny himself and take up his cross and follow me."

The table on the next page gives an overview of the course.

	EXPLORE	TALK / DVD	TALKBACK
WEEK 1	Mark 1:1	***CY*** It's Worth Exploring	Discuss Talk
WEEK 2	Mark 2:1-12	***CY*** Jesus Matters	Discuss Talk / DVD
WEEK 3	Mark 12:28-31	***CY*** Jesus Came	Discuss Talk / DVD
WEEK 4	Mark 8:27-33	***CY*** Jesus Died	Discuss Talk / DVD
WEEK 5	Mark 10:17-22	***CY*** God Accepts Us	Discuss Talk / DVD
WEEK 6	Mark 15:42 - 16:8	***CY*** Jesus Lives	Discuss Talk / DVD
CY We're Not Alone WEEKEND / DAY AWAY		***CY*** It's Tough to Follow Jesus ***CY*** You Need the Holy Spirit ***CY*** The Church is Your Family ***CY*** It's Good to Talk	Discuss Talk Discuss Talk Discuss Talk Discuss Talk
WEEK 7	Mark 1:14-15	***CY*** We Should Believe	Discuss Talk / DVD

Throughout the course, as you communicate the gospel to your young people, here are some things to keep in mind.

GET TO KNOW THEM

Young people place enormous emphasis on relationships, so get to know them as well as you can.

This doesn't mean that youth work involves "becoming like" young people, but it does mean that youth work is about taking time to get to know them as people.

GET ALONGSIDE THEM

One way to develop a relationship with a young person is to get alongside them through what they enjoy doing outside school. Whether it be sports or computer games, look to get into the world of a young person.

Find out what makes them tick and, if it is wholesome, get to know them through it.

DON'T BE AFRAID TO HAVE FUN WITH THEM

Show them that you are a real person and are able to relax with them.

TAKE AN INTEREST IN THEM

Many parents think that teenagers are a nuisance and most adults steer clear of young people, but if you show that you care about them and are interested in them as individuals, that will go a long way towards getting the gospel across.

It is worth mentioning that although it appears natural, talking about their school day is probably not the favorite subject of a young person and so may be worth avoiding!

AS FAR AS POSSIBLE, TREAT THEM AS ADULTS

During the course, your young people will be asked to discuss serious subjects with maturity, so, as far as you are able, treat them as adults.

However, discipline problems can emerge when working with young people. If you do face a difficult individual or situation, try the following:

- Be clear about what is acceptable and unacceptable in that situation. Young people appreciate clarity. (It is probably not a good idea to set out general "ground-rules" at the start of the course, as they may feel like they are back at school.)
- Take them to one side and don't confront them in front of their friends. Describe what they are doing and why it is a problem.
- Don't be afraid to deal with a problem if someone or something becomes a constant distraction. Few people enjoy confrontation, but if someone is disrupting a discussion, you need to remember that they are jeopardizing a gospel opportunity.

ABOVE ALL, TREAT THEM WITH CARE

You need to be aware that your friendliness is open to misinterpretation by young people and their parents. Make sure that there is not "even a hint... of any kind of impurity" (Ephesians 5:3) in anything you do or say.

It is unwise to speak alone with a young person out of view of other people, even if you're praying with them.

In addition, there will also be health and safety and/or child protection laws that you'll need to be familiar with. Make sure you know what these are and abide by them.

TRAINING NOTES
BEFORE THE COURSE

A well prepared ***CY*** leader will be dedicated in two particular areas: they'll be dedicated to the Bible and dedicated to prayer.

- **Dedicated to the Bible**

  The Bible is God's word. Whenever we open the Bible, God addresses us. In Hebrews 4:12 we read: "For the word of God is living and active. Sharper than any double-edged sword, it penetrates even to dividing soul and spirit, joints and marrow; it judges the thoughts and attitudes of the heart." Nothing else can do this.

  Because we're convinced of the power of God's word, our focus should always be on opening the Bible with young people.

- **Dedicated to prayer**

  Paul encourages the Christians at Colosse to devote themselves to prayer – in particular to pray for him in his evangelism. In Colossians 4:2–3 he says, "Devote yourselves to prayer, being watchful and thankful. And pray for us, too, that God may open a door for our message..." Before, during and after the course, we must pray.

  Mobilize others to pray too. Evangelism is a spiritual battle, so ask other Christians to pray for you and for your group. Report back to them regularly so that they can pray for specific needs and be encouraged by answered prayer.

With those two points in mind, there are a number of things you should do before the course starts.

GET TO KNOW MARK'S GOSPEL AND THE USER GUIDE

Read Mark at least three times and familiarize yourself with the *User Guide* section of this book. You will feel much more confident to lead participants once you've prepared yourself for the Bible studies and discussions that make up the course.

GET TO KNOW YOUR FELLOW LEADERS

It is important that people not only hear the gospel explained clearly, but also see it modeled in the life of believers.

You will be praying, studying and teaching young people together, so it's important to get to know each other and pray for each other before you begin. Your unity and love for one another will speak volumes about the truth of the gospel message.

PREPARE YOUR TESTIMONY

"Always be prepared to give an answer to everyone who asks you to give the reason for the hope that you have. But do this with gentleness and respect..." (1 Peter 3:15).

A testimony is an account of God's work in your life. Everybody who has been born again and who is becoming like Christ has a unique, interesting and powerful testimony, regardless of whether or not it appears spectacular.

At some point during the course, you may feel it appropriate to share your testimony with the group. Often someone will ask you directly how you became a Christian and you will want to have an answer ready.

- **Focus it.**
  Keep pointing to Christ, not yourself.

- **Structure it.**
  It may help to plan your testimony under these headings:
  My background (something about your family and how that shaped you);
  How I used to think (don't dwell so much on the sinful things you used to do, but rather on what you believed about God, the world, and yourself);

How I heard the gospel and my reaction to it;

How God changed me (how you responded to Jesus' call).

- **Personalize it.**
  Include one or two personal anecdotes to bring it to life. Keep it honest and interesting.

- **Time it.**
  Keep it short – if it's over 3 minutes it's probably too long!

Use the space below to prepare your testimony. You might find it useful to share your testimony with other leaders so that you can get feedback.

PRAY

- that those invited will attend the course.
- that God would enable you to prepare well.
- for the logistics of organizing the course.
- for good relationships with your co-leaders and young people.
- that God would equip you to lead faithfully.
- that the Holy Spirit would open the blind eyes of those who attend.

Take time now to pray through the points above.

TRAINING NOTES
DURING THE COURSE

A typical week at ***CY*** looks like this:

Food	30 minutes
Group Activity	25 minutes
EXPLORE	25 minutes
Talk / DVD	20 minutes
TALKBACK	20 minutes

FOOD

Eating together is an important part of each week at ***CY*** as it helps people to get to know each other and feel comfortable in the group. And you don't have to be sitting formally at a table for the meal to work well!

Take the lead in introducing people to each other.

Try to avoid theological discussions during this time. The intention is to share life, not to be spiritually intense.

The mealtime is not an opportunity to buttonhole individuals, although if an opportunity arises naturally for you to talk about your faith, you should take it.

GROUP ACTIVITY

The activities are designed to tie into the theme of each week. It is important that they do not dominate but are integrated into everything else in the course.

Make sure everyone is involved in the activity – including you!

EXPLORE

EXPLORE is a short Bible study from Mark's Gospel. [*See pages 106–108 for an example of this.*]

Sit where you can see everyone. That way, you can make eye contact with people, and it also ensures that they can see you too. It's not a good idea for leaders to sit next to one another, as it can look intimidating.

Because the theme of the group activity is designed to tie in with EXPLORE, try to refer to what was learnt during the activity.

During EXPLORE, your responsibility as a leader is more than just asking the Bible study questions. You should try to maintain a relaxed atmosphere and involve everyone in the discussion if possible. Try to avoid using Christian jargon that might confuse your group. And don't forget how important the tone of your voice and your body language can be as you lead the study.

It is important to listen carefully to the answers given by participants and to reply graciously. Young people need to know that they are valued and that their opinions are important to you.

Encourage your young people to write down the answers in the space provided in their *User Guide*. If they write things down, they are more likely to remember them.

The answers are provided for you in this book, although it is vital to prepare for EXPLORE by reading and thinking through the questions yourself in advance.

If you are asked a question that you don't know the answer to, don't panic. Offer to think about the question, do some research, and get back to the person next week. Write the question down and seek help from a good book or another leader. See www.christianityexplored.com/reading for recommended reading.

You should be able to complete the study in 25 minutes, but if you are behind schedule, don't feel you have to rush through the questions. If participants are stuck on some aspect of the Bible study, either from Mark or from somewhere else, feel free to discuss these things instead, if the group is interested. You can always finish the study during TALKBACK, if you like.

TALK / DVD

After EXPLORE, a talk is presented or a DVD is shown.

After you've heard the talks or watched the DVDs a few times, it can be tempting to listen less attentively! But be aware that the group is likely to follow your lead, and stop listening too.

TALKBACK

TALKBACK is an opportunity to respond to the issues raised during the talk / DVD. Use the questions provided to help your group unpack the truths that have been presented. [*See pages 109–110 for an example of this.*]

Again, it is not important to finish all the questions. They are just an aid to discussion. Add your own supplementary questions as necessary to ensure that participants have grasped the issues, and always try to direct attention back to the Bible.

As with EXPLORE, the aim is to allow young people to discover Christ through Mark's Gospel; to encourage and guide discussion, rather than to lecture. As a general rule, they should be talking more than you are!

Encourage the group to ask questions and thank people when they ask helpful questions about a subject. This will promote discussion and openness in the groups.

Listen carefully to all questions and answers. They will give you a good indication of each person's understanding and spiritual maturity. A wrong answer will often reveal as much, if not more than, a right answer. And a question that is "off-topic" can expose the most pressing issue in a person's life.

Bear in mind that the questions participants raise may subtly indicate more fundamental objections to Christianity. For instance, if someone seems to have a problem believing that Jonah could have survived in a giant fish for three days, trying to give detailed examples of the regurgitation of human beings by large aquatic creatures is probably unwise. It would be better to see that the participant's real issue is most likely the general trustworthiness of the Bible, and deal with that.

Many questions in TALKBACK have personal applications. Depending on your group, participants may feel shy about answering these in front of others. Giving your own answer can encourage them to do so. Otherwise, feel free to ask participants to answer questions in their own *User Guide* rather than out loud.

ENDING THE WEEK

Always finish at the promised time. Good timekeeping develops trust in the group, and with their parents!

Let participants know that they are welcome to stay and talk further if they like. Time spent talking with young people after the study officially ends gives you a great opportunity to find out where individuals are in their understanding of the gospel.

Seek to explain what they have not understood. Encourage them by sharing your own testimony if appropriate. Help them to see the need for a personal response to Jesus Christ, but do not pressure them.

In other editions of ***Christianity Explored***, participants are encouraged to complete a "Home Study" which consists of a series of questions on a passage or a reading from Mark's Gospel. In developing ***CY***, we found that young people tended to view Home Study as homework and so it was rarely done. As a result, we recommend that you simply encourage your young people to read Mark's Gospel through the course. Don't set it as Home Study – just make it clear that reading Mark will help them to get the most out of ***CY***.

TRAINING NOTES
WHAT DO I DO IF...

...THERE'S SILENCE?

If a question is met with silence, don't be too quick to speak – people could be thinking about their answer or they could just be shy about speaking first.

If you sense that someone knows the answer, but is too shy to speak, try asking them by name as they will probably be glad to answer.

It might be appropriate to try a "game", asking them to raise their hand if they agree or disagree with certain answers as you give them.

You might also try offering some help with finding the answers; for example, you might say, "There's a clue at the end of verse 2".

...ONE PERSON ANSWERS ALL THE QUESTIONS?

Thank them for their answers. Try asking the group, "What do other people think?"

Sit beside the talkative participant the following week. That will make it harder for them to catch your eye and answer the questions.

If the situation continues, you may need to speak to the participant after the study, asking them to give others an opportunity to answer next time. (For example, "Thanks so much for everything you're putting in to the group. I wonder if you could help me with the quieter people...")

...SOMEONE GIVES THE WRONG ANSWER?

Don't jump to correct wrong answers. Try asking, "What would verse 2 tell us about that?" You could also ask, "What do others think?" to see if anyone else has a more helpful answer.

If necessary, don't be afraid to graciously correct a wrong answer that may mislead others. Say something like, "Thank you, that's an interesting point, but I'm not sure that's what's going on here."

Have further questions in mind to develop the initial answer, for example, "What did you mean by that?" or "What does everyone else think?" or "Where does it say that?"

If no-one is able to answer the question, give the correct answer, showing from the Bible passage why it is the right answer.

...PEOPLE DO NOT ENGAGE WITH DISCUSSION?

This is a common problem when working with young people. Try making eye contact with the person to get them involved again with the discussion.

You could try using an illustration or a story which relates to the subject of your discussion, as this will often draw people back in.

If you know the person reasonably well you could try asking a direct question to encourage them to participate.

Sometimes, people just don't want to engage that week. This will often change the following week. If the suggestions above don't work, focus on those who are interested in the discussion, making the most of the time with the participants who want to listen and engage.

...SOMEONE ASKS A DIFFICULT QUESTION?

Be wary of giving glib answers to difficult and searching questions. If you don't know the answer, be honest and say you're not sure. Offer to find out the answer for next week. You could also offer to lend them a book on the subject – see www.christianityexplored.com/reading for suggestions.

...SOMEONE ASKS A DISTRACTING QUESTION?

A question may be raised that does not relate to the study and will take the group off track. Offer to discuss the issue later with the person.

...SOMEONE IS DISRUPTIVE?

If someone is being disruptive, try first of all to get them back into the discussion. It might be necessary to talk to them later about why they are being disruptive. Often this is because they are frustrated by the content, or upset by the group they're in. Sometimes, "reassigning" the person to one of the other groups can turn a disruptive participant into an active one.

Deliberately stupid or silly answers can also be a disruptive influence. If it is appropriate, laugh with the group, then gently try to bring the discussion back on track. If the comments are inappropriate or repeated, speak with the person afterwards and ask them to hold back their comments during discussions.

...SOMEONE DOES NOT WANT TO DO THE ACTIVITIES?

Show enthusiasm and enjoyment yourself. This will encourage others to take part in the activities. Usually, non-interaction will change as people get to know you and the group, and begin to see that the activities are being enjoyed by everyone else.

...SOMEONE DOES NOT COME BACK?

Don't panic. Jesus' words in Mark 4:3–20 remind us that even when we're preaching the word faithfully, it doesn't always take root. There will be people who will not want to come back. We have to trust in God's sovereignty, that he will bring the people of his choosing to the course – and that he will keep them there.

If appropriate, contact them to see if they are okay, letting them know that you were sorry to have missed them. Be careful not to pressure them to come back if they don't want to attend.

...PARTICIPANTS MISS A WEEK OR MORE?

Welcome them back and, during the meal, summarize what they've missed. You could also offer to lend them the DVD from the previous week.

...THE PASTORAL ISSUE THEY CONFIDE IN ME IS ONE I AM NOT QUALIFIED TO DEAL WITH?

It's best not to try and deal with situations if you feel you are out of your depth. Encourage the person to see someone with more experience within your group or church (your pastor or a Christian counsellor). Offer to pray with them about the issue if that is appropriate.

Take care in promising confidentiality when working with young people. There are some things that you must disclose (such as abuse), so don't promise to keep something secret until you've heard what they want to tell you.

TRAINING NOTES
AFTER THE COURSE

Jesus warns us in the Parable of the Sower (Mark 4:3–20) that there will be a variety of responses to the preaching of the gospel.

What will you do for those for whom the message has "gone in one ear and out the other"?

How will you help the shallow enthusiasts to deepen their response?

How will you provide a support for those who are vulnerable to having their initial commitment squeezed out of them by the pressure of their families, friends or their own personal ambitions?

And how will you help young disciples to continue growing in their understanding, godliness and love?

It's vital to have a follow-up strategy in place for all your young people.

GIVE OUT FEEDBACK FORMS

Feedback forms, given out during the last week of the course, are a great way to challenge your young people to think about where they currently are with Christ, and to help leaders plan a way forward once the course is ended. [*See page 65 for an example feedback form.*]

STAY IN TOUCH

CY is not a conveyor belt that either ships young people into the Christian faith – or tips them off into the street outside.

Having spent seven weeks with your group considering profound and personal issues, you will know them well – and they will know you well. Under these circumstances, it would clearly be wrong to "drop" participants once the course comes to an end.

Plan to stay in touch with all the young people in your group, and arrange it with your co-leaders so that each person has at least one Christian who remains in touch with him or her.

ARRANGE FOLLOW-UP

There is an opportunity at the end of the course for participants to express their commitment to Christ with a prayer. But be wary of thinking that this is the end of your role. Jesus calls us not to get people to "pray the prayer", but to "make disciples" (Matthew 28:19).

If anyone in your group has made a commitment to Christ, help them lay firm foundations so that they will be able to persevere. Make sure that they get involved in some form of regular Bible study and some area of Christian service.

You should invite them to start coming along to church if they're not already attending regularly. It's a great idea to encourage them to meet with others beforehand and go as a group.

PRAY

A supremely Christ-like way of caring for people is to pray for them. Even after the course has ended, it is important to pray for all the members of the group.

For new believers, pray for growth, fruitfulness and joy. For those who have not yet made a commitment, pray that the Lord will have mercy on them and send his Holy Spirit to open their blind eyes.

Pray for yourself, for patience and wisdom as you wait for God's word to do its work.

IDENTITY, MISSION, CALL IN MARK'S GOSPEL

As a leader preparing to teach Mark, there's no substitute for reading through Mark's Gospel at least two or three times. And as you read, you'll begin to see that Mark is preoccupied with three great themes:

- Who is Jesus? (Jesus' identity)
- Why did he come? (Jesus' mission)
- What does he demand? (Jesus' call)

Every passage in Mark has something to say to us about one or more of those themes.

Broadly speaking, the first half of Mark (1:1 – 8:30) is taken up with the question of Jesus' identity: it starts by saying, "The beginning of the gospel about Jesus Christ, the Son of God" and ends with Peter's statement, "You are the Christ."

The second half of Mark's Gospel is largely taken up with the question of Jesus' mission, which is why it is so dominated by the cross.

By way of example, look at one of the most significant passages in Mark's Gospel – Mark chapter 8, verses 27 to 38 – and you'll discover all three themes (identity, mission and call) in quick succession. Let's take a few verses at a time.

IDENTITY

The dominant question in verses 27–30 is Jesus' *identity*. Who exactly is Jesus?

"Jesus and his disciples went on to the villages around Caesarea Philippi. On the way he asked them, 'Who do people say I am?' They replied, 'Some say John the Baptist; others say Elijah; and still others, one of the prophets.' 'But what about you?' he asked. 'Who do you say I am?' Peter answered, 'You are the Christ.' Jesus warned them not to tell anyone about him."

People had lots of theories about Jesus' identity, just as they do now: "Some say John the Baptist; others say Elijah; and still others, one of the prophets." But Jesus gets very personal in verse 29: "What about you?... Who do you say I am?"

Peter answers the question about Jesus' identity correctly: "You are the Christ." Jesus is not "one of the prophets" as some were saying. He is actually the Christ – the *fulfilment* of all prophecy.

But although Peter has Jesus' identity right, it's clear he hasn't yet understood Jesus' mission.

MISSION

Let's look at Mark 8:31–33 to discover Jesus' mission.

"He then began to teach them that the Son of Man must suffer many things and be rejected by the elders, chief priests and teachers of the law, and that he must be killed and after three days rise again. He spoke plainly about this, and Peter took him aside and began to rebuke him. But when Jesus turned and looked at his disciples, he rebuked Peter. 'Get behind me, Satan!' he said. 'You do not have in mind the things of God, but the things of men.'"

Here, for the first time, Jesus begins to teach them his mission – that he "must suffer many things and be rejected by the elders, chief priests and teachers of the law, and that he must be killed and after three days rise again".

Jesus doesn't leave any room for misunderstanding (he "spoke plainly about this") because he knows that the disciples – and most of the public – have a very different expectation of what the Christ would be like. He would be a triumphant king, marching in to claim his territory, trampling the enemy underfoot and ushering in a glorious new era for his followers. A Christ who suffered and died would have seemed like a contradiction in terms.

Peter clearly has this triumphal view of the Christ in mind when he takes Jesus aside and begins "to rebuke him". But Jesus' strong reaction shows just how necessary death is to his mission: "Get behind me, Satan!... You do not have in mind the things of God, but the things of men."

The idea that the so-called "Son of God" had to suffer and die is still a stumbling block for many people today. But if we're to understand Mark's

Gospel – and indeed the whole Bible – correctly, it is essential to grasp the true nature of Jesus' mission: he "must suffer" and "he must be killed" so that we can be forgiven.

If that is Jesus' identity and mission, what are the implications for his followers?

CALL

What is Christ's call? Let's look at Mark 8:34.

"Then he called the crowd to him along with his disciples and said: 'If anyone would come after me, he must deny himself and take up his cross and follow me.'"

Having just spoken to the disciples about his own death, he calls the crowd to him and says, "If anyone would come after me, he must deny himself and take up his cross and follow me." It is striking, and not a little disturbing, to see Jesus immediately turn his attention from the cross *he* must take up, to the cross *we* must take up.

First, if we are to follow him, Jesus tells us we must deny ourselves. It is not a natural thing for human beings to turn away from their natural self-centeredness and self-reliance, but that is Jesus' call. We cannot follow him unless we deny our own selfish instincts.

Second, we cannot follow Jesus if we are not prepared to take up our cross. We must be prepared to serve him – and others – to the point of giving up our lives. In effect, Jesus must be more important to us than life itself.

If that seems irrational, we need to hear what Jesus says next in verses 35–38: "For whoever wants to save his life will lose it, but whoever loses his life for me and for the gospel will save it. What good is it for a man to gain the whole world, yet forfeit his soul? Or what can a man give in exchange for his soul? If anyone is ashamed of me and my words in this adulterous and sinful generation, the Son of Man will be ashamed of him when he comes in his Father's glory with the holy angels."

The first reason to obey Christ's call is in verse 35: if we give up our life for him, we'll save it; and if we don't, we'll lose it. That's the amazing thing about Jesus – you give him your life, and you find it. People today are always talking about "finding themselves". Jesus is the answer to that quest.

Second, verse 36 says that even if we were to gain the whole world by rejecting Jesus, we would still lose the most important thing we have – our soul. That's a great reason for obeying Christ's call. What is the most important thing to us? Our college education, our career, our boyfriend / girlfriend, our family? Or is it our soul?

The third reason to obey Jesus' call is in verse 37. If we miss out on eternal life, there is nothing we can do to buy it back. No wealth we may have accumulated, no worldly popularity, no friends in high places can win back the soul we will lose by not obeying Jesus' call.

And the fourth reason Jesus gives for obeying his call is in verse 38. If we reject Jesus, then he will reject us when he returns as judge of the world. So if the future belongs to Jesus, then it makes perfect sense to give him our time, our resources, our lives, and our love.

So that's Jesus' identity, mission and call in Mark 8.

IDENTITY		MISSION		CALL
Who is Jesus?		Why did Jesus come?		What does Jesus demand?
Mark 8:27–30	→	Mark 8:31–33	→	Mark 8:34–38

Read through the whole of Mark's Gospel and decide whether each paragraph is about Jesus' identity, mission or call. Label each one "I", "M", or "C", remembering that some paragraphs may be a combination of two or three of the above.

GOD'S ROLE IN EVANGELISM - AND OURS

We need to distinguish between God's role in evangelism and our role. It's going to be incredibly frustrating if we try to perform God's role – because only the creator of the universe is able to do that.

Look at 2 Corinthians 4:1–6.

> "Therefore, since through God's mercy we have this ministry, we do not lose heart. Rather, we have renounced secret and shameful ways; we do not use deception, nor do we distort the word of God. On the contrary, by setting forth the truth plainly we commend ourselves to every man's conscience in the sight of God. And even if our gospel is veiled, it is veiled to those who are perishing. The god of this age has blinded the minds of unbelievers, so that they cannot see the light of the gospel of the glory of Christ, who is the image of God. For we do not preach ourselves, but Jesus Christ as Lord, and ourselves as your servants for Jesus' sake. For God, who said, 'Let light shine out of darkness,' made his light shine in our hearts to give us the light of the knowledge of the glory of God in the face of Christ."

GOD'S ROLE IN EVANGELISM

What is God's role in evangelism? God makes "his light shine in our hearts to give us the light of the knowledge of the glory of God in the face of Christ".

In other words, God enables us to recognize that Jesus is God. God makes it possible – by his Holy Spirit – for a person to see who Jesus is.

The beginning of 2 Corinthians 4:6 reminds us that God said, "Let light shine out of darkness." That is a reference to the miracle of creation in Genesis 1:3. This same God who brought light into the world at creation now shines light into the hearts of human beings, enabling them to see that Jesus is God. In other words, for people to recognize that Jesus is God, God must perform a miracle.

People do not become Christians just because we share the gospel with them. God must shine his light in people's hearts so that they recognize and respond to the truth of the gospel.

And we know from verse 4 that people can't see the truth of the gospel because "the god of this age has blinded the minds of unbelievers".

Here, Paul reminds us that we are in the middle of a supernatural battlefield. The reason so many reject the gospel is that the devil is at work, preventing people from recognizing who Jesus is.

The devil blinds people by making them chase after the things of this world, which are passing away and which cannot save them. Their concerns are confined to the here and now: their popularity, their family, their relationships, their material possessions. They are blind to anything beyond that.

As a result, they can only see Jesus in the here and now, perhaps as a great moral teacher; his eternal significance is completely obscured. And, according to verse 4, Satan is determined to prevent people from seeing "the light of the gospel of the glory of Christ, who is the image of God". Satan does not want people to recognize who Jesus is.

OUR ROLE IN EVANGELISM

What then is our role in evangelism? "We... preach... Jesus Christ as Lord".

The word "preach" can evoke negative images, but it derives from a word simply meaning "herald", someone who relates important announcements from the king to his kingdom. Our role is to tell people the gospel and leave the Spirit of God to convict them of its truth.

These verses also reveal the attitude we should adopt as we preach. We are to be like "servants for Jesus' sake." The word translated "servants" literally means "slaves" in Greek. Paul was determined to present Christ to others without any hint of self-promotion.

We must remember that the only difference between ourselves and an unbeliever is that God, in his mercy, has opened our blind eyes and illuminated our hearts by his Holy Spirit. We should be forever grateful, and so seek to promote Christ, not ourselves.

We must keep preaching Christ as Lord and, remembering that only a miracle from God can open blind eyes, we must keep praying that God will shine his light in the hearts of unbelievers.

2 Corinthians 4:1–6 also helps us to carry out our role in the right way: "we do not use deception, nor do we distort the word of God... by setting forth the truth plainly we commend ourselves to every man's conscience in the sight of God... For we do not preach ourselves, but Jesus Christ as Lord".

When we tell people about Christ, we should demonstrate the following qualities:

- **Integrity** – "we do not use deception". We are straight with people; we are genuine and sincere.

- **Fidelity** – we do not "distort the word of God". We have to tell people the tough bits. If – for example – we don't tell our young people about sin, about hell, and about the necessity of repentance, then we are distorting God's word. Preaching these hard truths means trusting in the work of the Holy Spirit to draw people to Christ, however "difficult" the message.

- **Humility** – "we do not preach ourselves, but Jesus Christ as Lord". We must draw people to Jesus, not to ourselves. We must always remember that young people are easily impressionable, and that we want them to make a decision to follow Christ because they are convinced by the truth, and are being led by the Holy Spirit, rather than being manipulated by their admiration of the youth leader.

As we use ***CY*** to preach the gospel, we must remember that it is up to God whether somebody becomes a Christian or not. Only he can open blind eyes, so we must trust him for the results. God will do his part, and we must do ours.

This section contains the studies to work through over the seven-week course. It contains all of the material in the participant's *User Guide*, together with activities and answers to the questions.

SECTION 3
USER GUIDE

WEEK 1
CY IT'S WORTH EXPLORING

Welcome the group to the evening and thank them for coming. Introduce yourself if necessary, letting them know that you are there to help and answer any questions they might have.

GROUP ACTIVITY : "SIGNATURE BINGO"

Aim: To get everyone to know each other and to "break the ice".

Equipment: Pieces of paper (one for each member of the group) divided into 9 squares; pens; small bag; small strips of paper; 2 small prizes for winners; a CD player (optional).

- Give every participant a strip of paper and a pen. Ask them to write their own name on the paper and put it in the bag.
- Next, give every participant a piece of paper divided into 9 squares.
- Ask them to fill their grid with signatures from other people, putting one signature in each of the nine squares. If appropriate, play music in the background – you could fit this part of the activity to the length of one particular CD track – make sure it's only about 3 minutes long to add some urgency to the task, and to make sure things don't drag.
- Once you have given them time to get signatures, take out the bag.
- Tell the group that you are going to play bingo with their names, and that a prize will be awarded for the first completed line and the first completed card.
- Take the names out one at a time, and as you call out someone's name ask them to say "hello". At the same time, if someone has this name on their card they can cross it out. Once someone has a line they can call "bingo".
- Have a prize ready for the first completed line and first completed card.

Note: If the group is too large, it might be necessary to play this game in table groups, rather than with the whole group.

EXPLORE

▶ *Hand a* User Guide *to each participant. Ask them to turn to page 4 and to write down their answer to this question:*

If you could ask God one question, and you knew it would be answered, what would it be?

▶ *Ask the group to share their answers and note down what they are so that you can deal with them at some point during the course. Don't attempt to comprehensively answer all the questions at this time, although it is a good idea to acknowledge every question and assure participants that they will be covered during* **CY**. *(Some questions will be answered by the talks and some – like questions about suffering – are best dealt with after the talks on the cross / grace.) However, do try and answer at least two questions at this point. You might also want to write your own answer and share it with the group.*

▶ *Give the group one large piece of paper and some pens. Ask them to draw a poster of things that come into their minds when they think of Christianity. For example, they might draw a large cathedral or church. Note: Leaders need to allow the group to draw what they want. If they want to draw something that is theologically problematic, allow them to do it because there will be an opportunity later to correct misunderstandings.*

Give each person a Bible. Show them where they can find Mark's Gospel. Explain how chapters and verses work.

Ask everyone to turn to **Mark 1:1**.

One of the leaders should read **Mark 1:1** *aloud, then the group should work through the questions below. The answers are given here for your reference.*

What does Mark say Christianity is all about in the first sentence of his book?

He says that it is "good news". (You will need to explain that the word "gospel" means "good news".)

He says it's about Jesus.

He says it's about Jesus being the Son of God.

How is that different from some of the pictures we have drawn?

This question is designed to tackle some of the common misconceptions about the Christian faith that may have come up in the poster drawing exercise.

He says that it is "good news". In other words – it is not boring! If you think Christianity is boring, then you've not really understood what it's all about.

He says it's about Jesus. It's not about buildings, or services, or "religion" – it's about a man who lived and walked and breathed in history called Jesus.

He says it's about Jesus being the Son of God. It's about God making himself known to us through Jesus.

Deliver the talk. The recap (called UPLOAD) below appears in the participant's User Guide *for their reference.*

UPLOAD

- Christianity is not about rules or ceremonies. It's all about Jesus Christ.
- If we are here by chance we have no significance or value. But God created us – so we matter.
- Real living is not to be found in money, music or human relationships – it is found in a relationship with God.
- But how can we get to know God? We need him to introduce himself. According to Mark, that's exactly what God has done. In order to introduce himself to us, God has become a man: the person we call Jesus Christ.
- That's why "the gospel about Jesus Christ" is good news.

TALKBACK

Use the questions below to encourage discussion (they are also printed in the participant's User Guide*).*

Remember that this is the first week, and the aim here is not to explain the whole gospel, to challenge them to become Christians, or start an argument about what they currently believe. It is simply to open up the themes that will be covered in subsequent weeks.

Make sure TALKBACK does not run over time. It is much better to stop a good discussion, leaving them hungry for more, than to talk everything out in detail with the risk of boring some of the group, or putting them off coming back next time.

If you asked a group of people in the street: "What is the point of life?", what kind of answers would you get?

Answers might include: making lots of money; having a good time; having good friends; finding love.

You might ask them why they think different people think different things are important.

The aim here is not to criticize these views, but to get the group thinking about the meaning of life. Each of these views will be shown to be ultimately empty in the talks and discussions in the weeks that follow. There is no pressing need to comment on them now, unless the discussion naturally heads that way.

What do most people think about God and Christianity? Why do you think that is?

This is to recap the EXPLORE questions, without getting too personal. Answers may include: boring, irrelevant, outdated, repressive, controlling, moralizing etc.

Explain that churches can very easily forget what Christianity is all about – Jesus – and the resulting religion can become any or all of those things. But this is not real Christianity.

It is important to sympathize with anyone in the group who may have had a bad experience of religion – an unhelpful minister, boring or rigid services etc.

What about Jesus? Do people think he matters? What do *you* think?

At this stage don't press anyone to give an answer for what they think, but if they do, it may be appropriate to ask them why.

Remind them that, according to Mark 1:1, Jesus is "good news".

WEEK 2
CY JESUS MATTERS

Welcome the group and thank them for coming.

Recap on the previous week: I hope you can remember what we said last week. It was very simple, yet incredibly important. Christianity is not about beautiful buildings and boring services – it is all about Jesus Christ.

Remember Mark chapter 1, verse 1? "The beginning of the gospel about Jesus Christ, the Son of God."

But what was Jesus really like? Well, that's what we're going to look at this week.

GROUP ACTIVITY : "GUESS WHO?"

Aim: To show that a person's qualities reveal their true identity.

Equipment: PowerPoint; projector; slide show which you can make yourself or download from www.christianityexplored.com/cy; a prize. (Alternatively, if you don't have access to a projector, you can simply read the clues from the slides out loud.)

- Each PowerPoint slide contains five pieces of information (clues) about famous people. The clues are revealed one by one.
- Each team has to try and guess who is being described on the slide.
- The teams score according to how soon they guess correctly:

After clue 1	10 points
After clue 2	8 points
After clue 3	6 points
After clue 4	4 points
After clue 5	2 points

- The team with the most points wins the prize.

For Small Groups: Play with 2 teams and allow each team to guess *once* after each clue. The team who guesses correctly then gains the points. (Even after a team guesses correctly, you should still display the remaining clues and read them out loud.)

For Larger Groups: Give each table group leader the identities of the people on each slide so that they can score for their team. (This is so that once another team guesses the identity of the famous person, other teams can still continue to guess the person). Make it clear that each table can only have one guess per clue. Get the scores from each table leader and announce the winner.

Tip: Update the famous people on the slide show to keep it current and relevant for the location and age of the group.

At the end of the activity, say to participants: "Once you get all the facts about a person you can tell who they are. This week we're going to get some facts from Mark's history so we can find out who Jesus really is."

EXPLORE

Hand each participant their User Guide. *Ask them to turn to page 8 and to write down their answer to this question:*

Think of your best friend. What do you really like about them?

Ask a few participants to share their answers, then point out: "Isn't it interesting that most of you wrote down things about your friend's personality and how they behave, rather than commenting on the way they look? It's those things that make our friends important to us.

Do you know that we don't actually have a physical description of Jesus? But we do know a lot about his personality and what he did, and we're going to look at that this week. Because those qualities tell us some important things about him."

Ask everyone to turn to **Mark 2:1–12**. *Ask someone to read the passage aloud and then work through the questions below with the group.*

Why is the house full at the start of this passage? (look at Mark 1:45 for clues)

People wanted to come and meet Jesus.

He already had a reputation because he had healed the sick and because his teaching was worth hearing.

Imagine you are in the room. How would you have reacted to Jesus saying, "Son, your sins are forgiven"? (see verse 5) Why do you think he said it?

The man's immediate need appears to be that he should be healed physically.

However, Jesus knows that the man's greater need is that he should have his sins forgiven and so he deals with this need first.

Why do the religious leaders react so strongly when Jesus forgives the man's sin? (see verse 7) Do you think that their response is right?

They know that sins can only be forgiven by God and so for Jesus to forgive sins is to claim that he is God.

Because sin offends God, only God can forgive it.

The religious leaders are partly right, in that only God can forgive sin. But they are also wrong because Jesus is not blaspheming: he really is God.

Why does Jesus heal the man so that he can walk? (look at verse 10 for a clue)

Jesus does this to prove that he really does have authority to forgive sins.

No-one can see that the man's sins have really been forgiven, because something has happened *internally* to the man's relationship with God. So Jesus does something *visibly* miraculous to show that he really does have the power to forgive him.

Deliver the talk or watch the DVD. The recap below appears in the participant's User Guide *for their reference.*

UPLOAD

- Mark claims that Jesus is the Son of God. He then describes five events to show that this is true:
- Jesus' authority to teach – **Mark 1:21–22**
- Jesus' ability to heal – **Mark 1:29–31**
- Jesus' control of nature – **Mark 4:35–41**
- Jesus' power over death – **Mark 5:35–42**
- Jesus' authority to forgive sins – **Mark 2:1–12**

TALKBACK

Use the questions below to encourage discussion:

Which of the five events that Mark records would you have found most amazing or scary? Why?

This question is designed to get the group talking about the actual events that have been described by Mark and explained by the talk.

As they are talking about it, try to get them to see the difference between the amazement they would experience seeing a magic trick, say, and the disturbing shock of seeing the things that Jesus did – disturbing because of what they reveal about Jesus.

What do you think of Jesus?

This is a more direct question, although it is okay for people to reserve judgement at this stage by saying, "I'm not sure yet." As the weeks go on, the evidence will become more compelling.

It may be appropriate at this stage to show why it is simply not right to say that Jesus was "just" a good man, or a teacher, or a religious leader – he must either be a fake, a lunatic or exactly who he claims to be.

If you have time, now is the moment to answer another of the questions that were asked in the first week's EXPLORE: "If you could ask God one question, and you knew it would be answered, what would it be?"

Make sure that you do not over-run on time. It's always better to leave them wanting more and eager to return next week.

WEEK 3
WHY JESUS CAME

Welcome the participants.

Recap on the previous week: As we flicked through the opening chapters of Mark, we saw Jesus amazing the crowds with his teaching, curing diseases with a touch, calming a storm with a word, raising the dead, and we even heard him claim to be God by saying that he had authority to forgive sin.

So, all the evidence in Mark's Gospel suggests that Jesus was a man with the power and authority of God himself.

This week we are going to explore what Jesus said about himself a little more.

GROUP ACTIVITY : "WRONG SKETCH"

Aim: To show that everything has a particular purpose.

Equipment: Various household items (e.g. a broom, a toothbrush, a wooden spoon, a bucket etc.)

- Give each group some items and ask them to prepare a 30 second sketch that makes use of all the items. The only proviso is that the items cannot be used as they would normally be used.
- Get them to perform the sketches to the group.

Example: A possible sketch could be a person coming into a hairdressers, having their hair brushed with a broom and using the spoon as a mirror.

At the end of the activity, say to participants: "Everything has a proper purpose, doesn't it? If we get that wrong, things look ridiculous. So this week we're going to find out Jesus' true purpose. We're going to see why Jesus came."

EXPLORE

Hand each participant their User Guide. *Ask them to turn to page 12 and to write down their answer to these questions:*

What do you think is the biggest problem facing the world?

Ask the group to share their answers and discuss as appropriate. When possible problems are suggested, see if other members of the group agree and if not, ask them why not.

From last week's *CY*, what does Jesus think is the biggest problem facing the world?

Get the answer from the group.

In Mark 2:1–12 we saw that Jesus did not deal first with the man's paralysis but with his sin. According to Jesus, the biggest problem facing the world is our sin.

▶ *Ask everyone to turn to* **Mark 12:28–31**. *Ask someone to read the passage aloud and then work through the questions below with the group.*

What does it mean to love God with all your heart, with all your soul, with all your mind and with all your strength?

This means that we put God first in our lives. No-one and nothing else can take God's place. (Note: It may be helpful to give a concrete example of what that means by turning to the first part of the ten commandments, Exodus 20:1–11. For example, you could refer people to Exodus 20:7 and talk about whether your group have ever misused God's name.)

What does it mean to love your neighbour as yourself?

It means that we should treat other people as we would like to be treated ourselves. (Note: It may be helpful to give a concrete example of what that means by turning to the second part of the ten commandments, Exodus 20:12–17. For example, you could refer people to Exodus 20:16 and talk about whether your group have ever lied to someone.)

Notice that Jesus is not only interested in the way we seem outwardly, but the way we are deep down, in our hearts and minds.
(see Matthew 5:21–22; Matthew 5: 27–28.)

How good do you think you are at living up to these two commands? Where do you especially fall down?

This question is designed to help the group see that everyone falls short of these two commands – the two most important of God's commands according to Jesus.

You could get the discussion going by admitting that you yourself find it difficult always to obey these two commands. (You probably shouldn't get too specific!)

Deliver the talk or watch the DVD. The recap below appears in the participant's User Guide *for their reference.*

UPLOAD

- Jesus did not come simply to be a moral example or to be a great teacher. He came to deal with our biggest problem: our sin **(Mark 2:17)**.

- To sin means to reject God and to put other things in his rightful place.

- We have all rebelled against God in this way.

- If we continue as we are, Jesus warns us that our sin will lead us to hell **(Mark 9:43–47)**. Only Jesus can rescue us.

TALKBACK

Use the questions below to encourage discussion:

What are some of the reasons that people give for why Jesus came? What do you think?

This question extends the discussion from the last two weeks about Jesus' identity and mission. The discussion should show that any of the common answers, like "to teach", "to show us how to love" etc are inadequate. Jesus repeatedly says he came to deal with our sin.

Do you think sin is a problem? Why or why not?

Some group members may not recognize that sin is a problem *for them.* The next question should help.

How would you feel if all your thoughts, words and actions were on display for everyone to see?

The aim here is to help them understand that sin is a problem for them personally.

Their sin is a problem: to others (who are hurt by and have to deal with our selfish behavior); and, most importantly, to God (who will rightly judge us for how we have lived.)

In other words, we all break the two most important commands: we all fail to love God and our neighbour as we should.

If you have time, now is the moment to answer another of the questions that were asked in the first week's EXPLORE: "If you could ask God one question, and you knew it would be answered, what would it be?"

Welcome the participants.

Recap on the previous weeks: We now understand who Jesus is and why he came. We saw last week that Jesus came to deal with our biggest problem: our sin.

This week we'll see how he does that.

GROUP ACTIVITY : "CELEBRITY PAIRS"

Aim: To show that we associate certain symbols with certain people.

Equipment: A prize; 18 pieces of paper: 9 with famous people on them and 9 with their associated symbols on them. (For example, you could match Neil Armstrong with the moon, Bill Gates with a computer, the Wright Brothers with a plane.)

- Split the group into two teams. The object of the game is to match the famous people to the relevant symbols.
- Place all 18 "cards" face down.
- The teams take it in turns to choose two cards and, if they are not a matching pair, the cards are turned back over.
- 10 points are awarded for each correctly matched pair. The game ends when all pairs have been matched. The team with the most points wins a prize.

Note: For large groups each table will need their own set.

At the end of the activity, say to participants: "We associate different symbols with different people. The cross is often associated with Christians or Jesus, but do we really understand what actually happened at the cross?"

EXPLORE

Hand each participant their User Guide. *Ask them to turn to page 16 and to write down their answer to this question:*

What would it be like to know when and how you will die? How would it make you feel? What would it lead you to do?

This is a question to get people talking. There are no wrong answers, so try to avoid making value judgements on their suggestions.

Most people would feel terrible knowing when and how they will die. It might make you desperate to try and avoid it (like in *Sleeping Beauty* when her father banned spinning wheels from the land because she was cursed to die by pricking her finger on one). Or else you could go mad, do nothing or perhaps "eat, drink and be merry..." Some people might devote the remaining time to helping others.

Note: Be aware that this question may be a particularly emotive issue for some of your group. Be extra vigilant for anyone who is troubled by this question, and make sure that you set an appropriate tone for the discussion. You should also offer comfort and support to anyone who is struggling with this issue.

Ask everyone to turn to **Mark 8:27–33**. *Ask someone to read the passage aloud and then work through the questions below with the group.*

What does Peter realize in verse 29?

Peter realizes that Jesus is the Christ – God's King in God's world. This is the first time that he sees this. This is pretty amazing, considering that he has been around Jesus all the time he was doing miracles, teaching and raising the dead.

Why would Jesus' words in verse 31 be surprising to Peter?

It would be surprising to hear that God's King was going to die. Peter has a "Superman" view of what it means to be a king.

Why does Jesus confront Peter in verse 32?

Peter is rebuked because he does not consider the "things of God" – in other words, he is looking at Jesus' Kingship from a human point of view, not God's point of view. He has realized who Jesus is, but he has not understood that Jesus' mission is to come and die.

When Jesus died on the cross, was it unexpected? (look at Mark 9:31 and Mark 10:33–34 for clues)

Jesus had taught his disciples repeatedly about the way he would die.

Deliver the talk or watch the DVD. The recap below appears in the participant's User Guide *for their reference.*

UPLOAD

- Jesus' death was no accident – it was planned.
- Jesus died to rescue us from the terrible danger we are in because of our sin – he died as "a ransom for many" **(Mark 10:45)**.
- When Jesus died, God's punishment for sin fell on him, so that it never has to fall on us.
- Jesus' death makes it possible for us to be accepted by God and enjoy a relationship with him.
- People have different reactions to Jesus' death: there are the busy soldiers; the proud religious leaders; the experience-seeking bystander; the crowd-pleasing Pontius Pilate; the centurion who recognizes that Jesus is "the Son of God".

TALKBACK

Use the questions below to encourage discussion:

How would you feel if someone else deliberately took the punishment for something you had done wrong?

This could bring out a number of differing reactions:

- Glad. The other person is a sucker for taking the blame.
- Guilty. I should have been punished instead.
- Bad. For the person who suffered.

Or any mixture of the above.

You could follow up with: "What if it is a really bad punishment – not just being told off by a teacher, but actually going to prison."

The question is designed to open up a discussion about guilt, responsibility etc, so there is no need to make any comment about the replies.

Why do you think Christians place so much emphasis on the cross?

Because the cross is where their sin was dealt with.

At the cross Jesus took the punishment we deserve. It should have been me dying there, but he died in my place.

If it weren't for the cross, no-one could *be* a Christian!

Which of the five reactions to Jesus' death do you most relate to?

Some people might not want to answer this in front of others. You could perhaps ask them to underline the one that refers best to them in UPLOAD.

Use any time you have left at the end to answer more of the questions that were asked in the first week's EXPLORE: "If you could ask God one question, and you knew it would be answered, what would it be?". This week on the cross may be the most appropriate moment to answer any questions about suffering.

*Tell the group about the "**CY** We're Not Alone" weekend / day away. Give a brief idea of what will happen and let them know that they will need their parents' permission to attend.*

WEEK 5

CY GOD ACCEPTS US

Welcome the participants.

Recap on the previous week: Last week we looked at how Jesus rescues us from our sin. He died on a cross as our substitute, in our place, taking the punishment that we deserve. We're in a desperate situation, we all face judgement, but Jesus paid the price for our sin so that we never have to.

This week, we're going to explore how that makes a difference to your life.

GROUP ACTIVITY : "SPAGHETTI TOWERS"

Aim: To illustrate what God's grace means.

Equipment: Long spaghetti; bananas; pears; two chocolate bars.

- Divide the participants into groups and give each group a packet of spaghetti, one banana and one pear. Tell them that they must build a tower 2 meters high using only these items. They can choose to have their banana or pear cut up by one of the leaders but once it is cut they are not allowed a whole piece of fruit again. Tell them that if they succeed, they win a chocolate bar.
- After a while, go to each group offering help. They will probably decline at first, but one group will ask for help eventually. (If no-one asks for help, become more and more keen to offer.) When the first group asks for help, tell them that the task is actually impossible to achieve, no matter how hard they try. Then tell them: "However, because you've asked for help, I'm going to give you two chocolate bars, as a gift."
- The game ends after a group asks for your help. That group is declared the winner and given two chocolate bars.

At the end of the activity, say to participants: "Some things are impossible for us to do, no matter how hard we try. The only way to get the prize in this case was to realize we couldn't do it, and admit it."

EXPLORE

Hand each participant their User Guide. *Ask them to turn to page 20 and to write down their answer to these questions:*

What things do people do in order to be accepted by others?

This question is intended to get the group thinking about acceptance.

It should become apparent that the world accepts people because they have achieved something or because they act or dress in a certain way. This is *conditional* acceptance. We are accepted because of something that we do, or say. When we stop doing that thing, we stop being accepted.

What things do people do in order to be accepted by God?

This question should reveal something about how people think they should approach and be accepted by God.

Typical answers might include: church attendance; being baptized; doing the right things; having Christians for parents.

Ask everyone to turn to **Mark 10:17–22**. *Ask someone to read the passage aloud and then work through the questions below with the group.*

Why does the rich young man think that God should accept him?

He claims that he has kept the commandments since he was a boy (verse 20). He thinks that God should accept him because he has kept this set of rules.

What is Jesus' response?

Jesus tells him that he should go and sell all he has and give money to the poor. And then follow him.

Why does the man leave? What does that show about the man?

The man leaves because he does not want to do what Jesus has asked him. He had a lot of money and chose this above following Jesus.

Jesus has shown the man that he has broken the very first commandment (see Exodus 20:2–3). He had made money into a god – it was more important to him than his Creator.

Like the man, people sometimes think they will be accepted by God because of good things they've done. But like the man, however good we think we are, we all put "things" in place of God (e.g. popularity, image, comfort, good grades, money etc).

Note: Jesus is not teaching that Christians should have no money. He is teaching that money should not take the place of God.

Deliver the talk or watch the DVD. The recap below appears in the participant's User Guide *for their reference.*

UPLOAD

- Most people think that God will accept them because of things that they have done or haven't done.
- The Bible tells us that God accepts us not because of anything *we've* done, but because of what *he* has done through Jesus.
- We cannot earn his forgiveness and we do not deserve it, but God accepts us when we have faith in Jesus.
- And that's grace: God treating us in a way we do not deserve because of what Jesus has done.

TALKBACK

Use the questions below to encourage discussion:

What exactly is grace? How would you explain it if someone asked you?

Grace is God forgiving us when we don't deserve it.

What do people find offensive about grace? What does it say about us?

It tells us that we are hopeless and helpless without it.

Many people hate this idea – we tend to be proud of ourselves and our own achievements.

If you have time, you could look again at the definition of grace in Ephesians 2:8–9.

What is so wonderful about grace? What does it offer us?

The free gift of eternal life. It offers us new life, freedom to follow God, a fresh start with Jesus in control, etc.

What does grace tell us about the character of God?

He is amazing! He is prepared to forgive me, welcome me as his friend, and he himself pays the price of my wrongdoing through the death of Jesus on the cross.

*Remind the group about the "**CY** We're Not Alone" weekend / day away. Give out invitations.*

WEEK 6

CY JESUS LIVES

Welcome the participants.

Recap on the previous week: Last week we saw that forgiveness is a gift, paid for by Jesus Christ. We don't deserve it, and we can't earn it. And that is grace: God treating us in a way we simply don't deserve. It's faith in what Jesus has done that saves us. Nothing else.

We've seen that Christ's death on the cross brings us forgiveness. This week, we'll look at how his resurrection affects us.

GROUP ACTIVITY : "STACK ATTACK"

Aim: This activity is intended to help participants see how important Jesus' resurrection is: without it, Christianity would fall apart.

Equipment: One tower of wooden blocks (there are numerous versions of this game available from toy stores).

- Participants take turns to remove a block from the tower, then place it on top of the tower.
- As the game continues, the tower becomes less and less stable until eventually it topples over.
- The person who removes the block that topples the tower loses.

Note: Make sure there is a time limit on this activity by allowing a maximum of 10 seconds to remove each block.

At the end of the activity, say to participants: "All it takes is for one crucial block to be removed, and the tower falls. The reason we're talking about the resurrection of Jesus this week is because it is 'the crucial block' in Christianity."

EXPLORE

Hand each participant their User Guide. *Ask them to turn to page 24 and to write down their answer to these questions:*

How would you score the following statements? (0 = completely unconvinced, 10 = very sure)

☐ **Jesus is God.**

☐ **Jesus came to rescue us from our sin.**

This exercise is intended to help participants think through what they've learned. Don't force people to reveal what they have written, although if they are happy to disclose their scores, it is good to ask why they have scored themselves as they have.

What would be your first reaction if you heard of someone who had come back from the dead?

Ask the group to share their answers.

Most will respond that it is impossible, or certainly not believable: dead people do not come back to life again.

A follow-up question could be to ask, "What would you need to know in order to be convinced that someone had actually risen from the dead?" If people say, "I'd need to see it myself", you might respond, "What if someone you trust had seen it, like a close friend or an eye-witness in a court case?"

Ask everyone to turn to **Mark 15:42 – 16:8**. *Ask someone to read the passage aloud and then work through the questions below with the group.*

Why are the women worried as they approach the tomb? (see Mark 16:3)

They do not know how they will move the stone.

What four things surprise them when they arrive? (see verses 4–6)

1. The stone is rolled away.
2. Jesus is not there.
3. A man in white greets them inside the tomb.
4. He tells them that Jesus is risen.

Should they have been surprised by Jesus' resurrection? (look at Mark 8:31, 9:30–31, 10:32–34 for clues)

In all of these passages, Jesus predicts that his resurrection will happen three days after he has been killed.

The women should not have been surprised by Jesus' resurrection. In fact, they should have expected it.

Why do you think the women ran away from the tomb?

They were amazed that Jesus had risen from the dead, but they were also afraid because they did not expect it.

They came looking for "Jesus the Nazarene" – a man from Nazareth – rather than "Jesus Christ, the Son of God".

Deliver the talk or watch the DVD. The recap below appears in the participant's User Guide *for their reference.*

UPLOAD

- The truth of the claims of Jesus rest on whether he rose from the dead.
- Jesus did die: Pontius Pilate, the Roman centurion, the soldiers, Joseph of Arimathea, the religious leaders and the women were all certain he was dead.
- Jesus did rise: the tomb was empty; no-one could produce the body; he was seen by hundreds of different people at different times, many of whom were later executed for insisting he was alive.
- The resurrection means we can have confidence that, if we trust in Jesus, God will raise us from death.
- The resurrection also proves that Jesus will come again as judge of the whole world **(Acts 17:31)**.

TALKBACK

Use the questions below to encourage discussion:

What part of the evidence for Jesus' resurrection do you find most convincing? Why?

This is to stimulate a general discussion on the evidence.

Encourage the group to think through the alternatives, e.g. "Couldn't Jesus have just fainted?" Answer: no – he'd been through torture, crucifixion and had been stabbed with a spear. The Romans were experts at this – killing was their business. Even if he had simply fainted – could he have rolled back the large stone, avoided a Roman guard and appeared fit and well to his followers soon after?

Do you think that Jesus rose from the dead?

Let people volunteer their answers.

But if anyone says "no" it's worth gently probing *why* they don't believe it. Is it that the evidence is not good enough – or is it because they are worried about the implications for them if it is true?

Why does Jesus' resurrection matter, if at all?

It matters, because if the resurrection happened as Jesus said it would, then we can trust Jesus on every other point. Jesus *is* who he says he is. Jesus *did* achieve what he said he would on the cross. Questions about life after death are no longer a matter of opinion – Jesus is able to answer the question, because he has been there and come back.

It also shows that Jesus rules over everyone and everything - even death - and proves that he will return to judge the whole world (Acts 17:31).

*Remind the group about the "**CY** We're Not Alone" weekend / day away. Give out schedules and encourage them not to miss it.*

WEEKEND / DAY AWAY

CY WE'RE NOT ALONE

This material should be covered on a weekend or day away. These sessions are very similar to the ones so far, except that there is no Bible study before the talk. It is good to allow longer for TALKBACK during these sessions.

CY WE'RE NOT ALONE
CY IT'S TOUGH TO FOLLOW JESUS

Welcome the participants and give a short overview of the schedule for the day or weekend: How would you prepare if you had to run a marathon? Apparently, you need to do two things. First, you need to find out all the details about the event to see whether you're up for the challenge. Then, you need to make sure you get proper training and have people who'll support you.

Well that's really what this weekend / day is about. We're going to find out what it means to be a Christian, to make sure we know the cost involved in following Jesus. Then we're going to look at how God enables people to live the Christian life. We're also going to be hearing from some real live Christians who'll be talking about their experiences.

GROUP ACTIVITY : "TOWERS AND TARGETS"

Aim: To convey the need to count the cost before trusting in Jesus.

Equipment: Use the same tower building blocks that you used for "Stack Attack" in Week 6; a whistle; two small kitchen sponges; a prize.

- Split the group into two teams, with one set of blocks each. The object of the game is to knock over the opposing team's tower by throwing a sponge at it. But first, each time has to decide how to build its own tower. The winning team will be the one whose tower is highest at the end of the game.
- The game takes 8 minutes: 2 minutes talking and planning time, during which each team decides which three players will throw a sponge, and how they will build their tower; 5 minutes building time; 1 minute during which the teams attempt to knock down their opponents' tower with three throws of the sponge (each thrower only has one throw).
- Blow a whistle after each time period is up.
- After the sponge is thrown, measure the towers and announce the winners – awarding whatever prize you think appropriate.
- You could repeat the exercise if you have time. Their experience from the first run through will make them assess things differently the second time round.

Hand each participant their User Guide. *Ask them to turn to page 28.*

Deliver the talk. The recap below appears in the participant's User Guide *for their reference.*

UPLOAD

- In Luke 14 Jesus describes a man building a tower and a king going to war. In both cases they must stop and think before making a big decision. Jesus says that those who want to follow him should do the same.

- If we are to follow Jesus we must be willing to suffer and put Jesus first in our lives.

TALKBACK

Use the questions below to encourage discussion:

What events make people suddenly change the way they live? What changes?

There are a lot of potential answers to this question. If no-one starts talking there are some suggestions below to get the discussion moving. Try to respond to their ideas by asking them what the positives and negatives would be in each case.

- Fall ill: can no longer play sport; stay at home; can't get a job; miss holidays; plenty of time to watch TV.
- Get married: can't date anyone I like; can't make decisions on my own; sharing your life with someone you love.
- Move house: new friends; new school; unfamiliarity.
- Inherit a fortune: no need to work; move house; buy what you want; have increased fears about security.

What sort of things would someone need to start doing if they followed Jesus?

Answers will include: reading the Bible, praying, going to church. But press the group to think about character, rather than activities. Jesus wants us to start loving, forgiving and serving people – because Jesus loves us, forgives us and has served us.

Make the point that doing these things is a joy, because you can trust Jesus to know what is best for your life.

What things would they need to stop doing if they followed Jesus?

Young people will often say obvious things like: stop swearing / getting cross with my brother / talking back to teachers or parents. But press them to see *why* these things have to stop. If you are a Christian you have a new master who you want to please. He hates these things, so you will hate them too.

And again, it's easier to do these things when we trust Jesus to know what's best for us.

Why would anyone bother choosing to live a life that is so hard and different from everyone else?

You might like to remind your group of the joys of following Jesus, e.g. the wonder of knowing God our Creator, the peace and assurance of sins forgiven, the purpose that comes from following Jesus, the certainty of eternal life, etc.

CY WE'RE NOT ALONE
CY YOU NEED THE HOLY SPIRIT

GROUP ACTIVITY : "GUIDE THE WAY"

Aim: To show that God leads his people by his Spirit.

Equipment: Blindfolds; baby's "shape sorter" puzzle.

- Split the participants into smaller teams of around four each.
- Give each group a blindfold. One person in each group should be blindfolded, and the others in their group are responsible for "directing" that person to do a particular task. Do not disclose the task until all the blindfolds have been put on.
- Tell the teams their task: "You must direct your blindfolded team member to pick up a block and put it in the correctly-shaped hole. You must not touch your team mate in any way, and the first one to complete the task wins."

At the end of the activity, say to participants: "It is impossible to live the Christian life without the Holy Spirit to guide you."

▶ *Hand each participant their* User Guide. *Ask them to turn to page 30.*

▶ *Deliver the talk. The recap below appears in the participant's* User Guide *for their reference.*

UPLOAD

- The Holy Spirit who comes to live in Christians is the Spirit of Jesus himself.
- He has a number of roles including:
  - guiding followers of Jesus
  - showing people their sin
  - changing people by giving them the desire to please God.
- Jesus promises that when we trust in him, he will come and live in us forever by his Spirit **(John 14:15–16)**.

TALKBACK

▶ *Use the questions below to encourage discussion:*

Before *CY*, what did you know about the Holy Spirit?

Use the opportunity to emphasize the main points of the talk, and to correct any wrong ideas.

What did you find most surprising about who the Holy Spirit is or what the Holy Spirit does?

Again, an opportunity to reinforce or extend some of the teaching from the talk.

How do you feel about Jesus' Spirit coming to live "with you" and "in you"? (John 14:17)

Individuals may feel scared about the idea of the Spirit living in them. Reassure them by telling them that he is the "Spirit of Jesus". In other words, it is Jesus who comes to live in them with all his goodness, love, and forgiveness. He wants what is best for you, and will guide you towards living that way.

CY WE'RE NOT ALONE
CY THE CHURCH IS YOUR FAMILY

GROUP ACTIVITY : "CAKE BAKE"

Aim: To show the importance of co-operation in the church family.

Equipment: You will need an oven nearby, and the following items gift-wrapped: a cook book with a cake recipe; a wooden spoon; scales; cupcake holders; the ingredients needed for the recipe; baking tray; bowl.

- Announce that they are going to bake cup-cakes. Give each participant one of the gift-wrapped items. Explain that each person is responsible for using their particular item during the making of the cup-cakes. They must cooperate with others since they are not allowed to use another person's item.
- Tell them to unwrap their item and get baking!
- Once the cup-cakes are in the oven, leave them to bake while you deliver the talk. You can then give them out at the end.

At the end of the activity, say to participants: "I hope you could see that if you didn't co-operate with each other, we wouldn't have been able to get the cakes in the oven."

Hand each participant their User Guide. *Ask them to turn to page 32.*

Deliver the talk. The recap below appears in the participant's User Guide *for their reference.*

UPLOAD

- In the Bible, "the church" is not a building but a group of Christians who follow Christ together.
- If we are to live the Christian life, we need to help each other.
- A good church will teach the Bible truthfully, encourage each other, remember Jesus' death and pray together.

TALKBACK

Use the questions below to encourage discussion:

What has been your experience of church? Was it positive or negative?

We need to recognize that many young people will have had an experience of church that is not positive.

This is the moment to apologize (if necessary) for the way that some adult Christians have been boring, or unhelpful or have not worked at communicating the gospel properly as they should. Churches are made up of sinful human beings like you and me, so it is not surprising that it goes wrong sometimes.

It may also be necessary to point out that some churches may not be real churches at all. They may have lost sight of the fact that Jesus saves them by God's grace, and think that they please God by their services, goodness and religious practices. It is not surprising that these churches are cold or harsh or boring – because they are not the real thing.

What do you think God's family *should* be like?

If the group has caught the vision for what church is for, and could be like, this should provoke a great discussion.

If particular grievances about the way your church operates come up, then write them down to discuss later – as a youth leadership team, or with your church leaders. But make sure that the group doesn't think that they can command the rest of the church to do things for them. They must encourage other Christians, just as much as other Christians encourage them.

Young people often respond very positively when given responsibility, so help them see that the church family is a great opportunity to really make a difference in other people's lives, e.g. by encouraging younger Christians.

What difference do you think a good church should make to someone who is trying to follow Jesus?

It should be the place where we find the love and forgiveness of Jesus, learn more about him and grow to be more like him.

Use the opportunity to share your testimony of how you have been helped by, and enjoyed the opportunity to contribute to, churches you have belonged to in the past. It's important to show how wonderful it is to be part of such a diverse but like-minded family.

CY WE'RE NOT ALONE
CY IT'S GOOD TO TALK

GROUP ACTIVITY : "TEAM CHARADES"

Aim: To demonstrate the importance of being able to speak to others.

Equipment: A list of words that can be acted out; a prize.

- Split the participants into teams of around 5–6 people each.
- Announce that you are going to play Team Charades.
- Explain that one person from each team will come to you to be told a particular word that they are to act out for their team. They must then act out the word without speaking or writing. If someone guesses the word correctly, they run to you and tell you the answer. You then give that person the next word on the list and they go back and act this out to their team.
- The game continues until one team wins by reaching the end of the list. Award that team a prize.

At the end of the activity, say to participants: "Aren't you glad that you don't have to communicate like that all the time?"

➧ *Hand each participant their* User Guide. *Ask them to turn to page 34.*

➧ *Deliver the talk. The recap below appears in the participant's* User Guide *for their reference.*

UPLOAD

- The Bible and prayer are vital to the Christian life. When we read the Bible, God talks to us. When we pray, we talk to God.
- The Bible enables us to be strong and keep going in the Christian life.
- Christians can pray to God about anything, knowing that he is in control of everything.

TALKBACK

Use the questions below to encourage discussion:

Have you read any parts of the Bible? What did you like about them? What did you find difficult?

Encourage the group to offer their favorite story, or Bible passage; tell them yours and why you find it so exciting.

People may say that they find the Bible difficult to understand. Encourage them to read the Gospels first. Explain too that this is why we have groups like this – to help with some of the more difficult things.

Some people may raise specific instances of things they find hard to believe. Offer to discuss these with them at some point during the weekend / day.

Do you ever pray? What kind of things do you say to God? When are you most likely to talk to God?

It's very rare for anyone to say they have never prayed. Listen to the answers carefully. It may then be appropriate to say: "How would you feel if someone treated you like that – only rang you up when they were in trouble or they needed something?"; "What would that say about that relationship?".

What do you think you might find most difficult about praying and reading the Bible?

Here are three areas that are worth focusing on:

- Opportunity: many young people find it hard to find the space and quiet – especially if they share a bedroom. Make suggestions for when and where they could set aside time to read and pray regularly.
- Keeping going: suggest Bible notes, meeting with small groups of friends to pray regularly for each other etc.
- Understanding: suggest an ongoing group Bible study that might be appropriate to them.

It may be useful to have Bible reading notes available to help anyone in your group who wants to begin reading the Bible for themselves.

WEEK 7
CY WE SHOULD BELIEVE

Welcome the participants to the final week.

Recap on the previous week: Last week we looked at Jesus' resurrection, and saw how it offers great hope in the face of death. He got through death so he can get us through it too. It also provides a great warning: there will be a judgement, and Jesus will be the judge.

This week, we're going to look at Mark chapter 8. From that chapter, we're going to find out exactly what it means to be a Christian.

GROUP ACTIVITY : "TANGRAMS"

Aim: To show that you need to put all the pieces together to make a complete picture.

Equipment: Set of Tangram pieces for each team (you can buy these from a toy store or download them from the internet); a prize; PowerPoint; projector; slide show which you can make yourself or download from www.christianityexplored.com/cy

- Split the participants into two or three teams and give each team a set of Tangram pieces. Display in turn each shape that they must try to make. Remind them that they must use all their pieces.
- Award the fastest team 10 points and the second fastest team 5 points for each of the shapes they make.
- Show the solution on the screen.
- The winning team is the one with the most points and wins the prize.

At the end of the activity, say to participants: "If we're to get the picture right, we have to put the pieces together in the right way. That's what we'll be doing this week as we put together all the pieces we've gathered over the past seven weeks."

EXPLORE

Hand each participant their User Guide. *Ask them to turn to page 36 and to write down their answer to this question:*

We started *CY* by asking: "If you could ask God one question, what would it be?" If God were to ask *you* one question, what would it be?

Ignore any silly answers. This question will reveal how much your group has absorbed over the last seven weeks. You might get things like:

- What is stopping you from believing in me?
- Why haven't you put your trust in Jesus?
- Why don't you tell others about me?

As this is the final week you should follow up by asking your group, "How would you answer that?"

Ask everyone to turn to **Mark 1:14–15**. *Ask someone to read the passage aloud and then work through the questions below with the group.*

What do you think Jesus means when he says: "the good news of God"?

This question helps to reveal if participants have understood what the gospel is.

It is the good news that Jesus, God's Son, came into this world, lived a perfect life, died for us on the cross, rose from the dead and is in heaven today, so that whoever repents and believes in him will be accepted by God and enjoy a relationship with him forever.

What does Jesus mean when he says: "the time has come" and "the kingdom of God is near"?

It is like saying, "This is it"; the time that everyone has been waiting for is here.

God's kingdom – his power and authority over everything – is breaking into this world and being shown in Jesus' life, death and resurrection.

What do you think the word "repent" means?

Repentance is a complete inner change of our attitude towards God and other people.

It begins with a sincere apology to God for our sin because we realize that it has offended him. We then turn from living our own way and start to live God's way.

That means being *for* what Jesus is *for*, and *against* what he is *against*.

What do you think it means to "believe the good news"?

Believe means more than just saying something is true. It means:

1. We know about Jesus and what he has done.

2. We are convinced that these things about Jesus are true.

3. We place our trust in Jesus and obey him.

Deliver the talk or watch the DVD. The recap below appears in the participant's User Guide *for their reference.*

UPLOAD

- In Mark chapter 8, Jesus' disciples have begun to see who he is. Peter recognizes Jesus as "the Christ", that is, the King promised in the Old Testament who would have the power and authority of God himself.

- Jesus then teaches them that he came to die. He knows that the only way sinful people can be brought back into a relationship with God is by dying in their place.

- Then Jesus says, "If anyone would come after me, he must deny himself and take up his cross and follow me". Denying self means no longer living for ourselves but for Jesus and for others. Taking up our cross means being prepared to follow him, whatever the cost.

- Jesus gives a convincing reason to live like this: "...whoever loses his life for me and for the gospel will save it" **(Mark 8:35)**.

TALKBACK

Use the questions below to encourage discussion:

How would you score the following statements?
(0 = completely unconvinced, 10 = very sure)

- [ ] **Jesus is God.**
- [ ] **Jesus came to rescue us from our sin.**
- [ ] **Following Jesus means denying ourselves and putting Jesus first, whatever the cost.**

These questions are designed to see how much the group has absorbed about the content of the Christian message over the weeks.

What choices will you make now that you've finished *CY*? What is the next step for you?

Write down everyone's answer so you can plan a way ahead and pray for them appropriately.

You need gently to encourage people to opt for one of two routes:

- "I need more time to think." Even if someone thinks that Jesus is definitely not for them, encourage them not to close the door but to keep putting themselves in the place where they will hear about Jesus and spend time with those who follow him. For others, who genuinely do not have enough information or need more time to absorb and think through the gospel message, the same encouragement is appropriate.
- "I would like to become a Christian." It would be good for anyone who has reached this point to see if they really understand what repentance means.

A prayer of commitment may be said with the whole group (see over).

WEEK 7

➤ *As this is the end of the course, expand upon the choices now available to participants. Don't forget to follow up with each of them (see "After the Course" in Section 2 of this book).*

➤ *Close by saying:* "Thank you for coming to ***CY***. I really hope you've enjoyed it. If you've become convinced of who Jesus is and what he came to do, and you understand what it will mean to follow him, you may want to echo the following prayer quietly in your own heart:

> **Heavenly Father, I have rebelled against you. I have sinned in my thoughts, my words and my actions – sometimes unconsciously, sometimes deliberately. I am sorry for the way I have lived and ask you to forgive me. Thank you so much that Jesus died on the cross so that I could be forgiven. Thank you that I can now see clearly who Jesus is and why he came. Please send your Holy Spirit so that I can follow Jesus whatever the cost. Amen.**

If you did pray that prayer, let me know – I'd love to help you get started as a Christian.

We really want to know what you thought of ***CY***, so that we can do it better next time. It would be great if you'd fill out this FEEDBACK FORM [*hand them out*]. Don't worry – your form will be treated with strict confidence, and not shown to anyone else. Well, that's it. I've really enjoyed the last seven weeks and I hope you have too."

CYA

CY: The Youth Edition of ***Christianity Explored*** was developed by Barry Cooper, Matthew Seymour and Sam Shammas in association with Young Life (UK).

Young Life exists to see Christian young people built up in their faith and reaching out with the gospel. Visit www.younglife.org.uk for more information.

Our grateful thanks go to the Young Life groups and numerous church youth groups who graciously piloted ***CY*** before it even became known as ***CY***. Your feedback has been invaluable.

The course has also been greatly enhanced by the contributions of Ruth Chan, Martin Cole, Joanna Cook, Richard John, Helen Thorne, Bob Willetts, Anne Woodcock and the exceptional Tim Thornborough.

Lastly, our thanks to Diane Bainbridge and Alex Webb-Peploe whose attention to detail and passion for the gospel shine through every page.